CW01402403

GOING PRIVATE

GOING PRIVATE

Privatisations Around the World

*David Clutterbuck with
Susan Kernaghan and Deborah Snow*

MERCURY

First published in 1991
by Mercury Books
Gold Arrow Publications Limited,
862 Garratt Lane, London SW17 0NB

Set in Melior by TecSet Limited

Printed and bound in Great Britain by
Mackays of Chatham PLC, Chaltham, Kent

British Library Cataloguing in Publication Data
Going private: Privatisations around the world.
  I. Clutterbuck, David   II. Kernaghan, Susan
  III. Snow, Deborah
  338.7

  ISBN 1–85251–014–5

CONTENTS

PREFACE

The international movement to return public sector activities to the private sector is as dramatic — perhaps more so — than the nationalisation process that preceded it. The story of privatisation is not one of dry statistics: it is composed of hundreds of stories of individual organisations, which had to relearn how to survive. Some were state monopolies, which have had to come to grips with the reality of competition from new domestic and international competitors, to whom they had to carry the commercial fight.

Some were manufacturing operations with but one customer — a state agency. Others were oil companies freed to operate competitively on an increasingly international market, or were loss-making firms that had been bought by the state in times of difficulty and were now draining the country's coffers. Still others were industries that had been considered strategically important. Following privatisation, these often had to comply with strict new regulations, designed to protect the national or the consumer's interest.

In France, for example, insurance and banking groups were among the first to regain private status after their nationalisation only a few years earlier by a Socialist government. To them, it was a question of realigning themselves to serve the market rather than the state.

What virtually all privatisations have in common is that the organisation has had to undergo radical and uncomfortable change to enable it to survive in the competitive world of the private sector. Some privatised companies such as the National Freight Consortium, which was immediately plunged into competitive markets, have adjusted rapidly while others such as British Telecom, which operates in a highly regulated near-monopoly market, have been under much less pressure to shed their public sector habits, although British Telecom has still made remarkable progress in this direction. The cases in this book explore how these organisations prepared for and made the necessary changes; how they coped with the complexities of transition from one sector to the other; and how they have fared since.

Reviewing these cases, and others which we have encountered in our researches, it is clear that there are several common problem areas, and every enterprise which considers following the privatisation route should take them into account. They include the following:

- The commitment of top management time to the mechanics of privatisation is invariably high. There is considerable danger that top management will neglect the business because its concentration is focused elsewhere. There is thus a strong need for a good second team to take over day-to-day running of the organisation.

- Some changes need to be made well before privatisation: for example, accounting procedures that budget against the bottom line and results, rather than simply allocate funds; and structural changes to put in place key functions such as marketing.

- A massive culture change is almost always necessary. Culture change takes time — a minimum of five years for an organisation of a few hundred people, far more for much larger enterprises. Substantial investment is often needed to retrain middle management, who often find it difficult to adapt to a commercial culture.

- Consumers expect a higher standard of service from privatised companies. Even if a corporation's performance improved, it often failed to keep pace with consumer expectations.

- Privatised companies often need drastic restructuring. Over 70 per cent of privatised companies said a far-reaching restructuring of management was required, but only 50 per cent of companies still in state ownership thought it would be needed, according to a survey of chairmen and chief executives carried out by United Research in 1990.

- Many newly privatised companies made the mistake of attempting to deal with their problems with a sequential approach. First they cut costs, before moving to make investments, thinning out management and improving customer service. The National Freight Consortium, on the other hand, cut costs at the same time as tackling customer service, marketing and the management structure.

- Senior managers, particularly of utilities, are more exposed and publicly accountable for the performance of their companies. Under public ownership, this responsibility lay somewhere between managers, civil servants and ministers.

- Achieving public commitment for the initial sell-off is essential to provide impetus to the newly-privatised company. This is often achieved by advertising campaigns followed by the allocation of a retail tranche.

INTRODUCTION

The Privatisation Phenomenon

The movement of enterprises between the public and private sectors is not a solely twentieth-century phenomenon. Throughout history, governments have brought elements of the economic infrastructure under their direct control and (occasionally) subsequently released them as their strategic or political importance wanes. In the nineteenth century the UK government (and many other governments) established powerful state-owned monopolies over the media — initially over the post, then, in the twentieth century, over the new medium of radio, then television. However, the explosive growth of public ownership in the twentieth century arose from very different ideological grounds than simply sustaining the power of the government of the day. Among the key reasons were:

- The basic socialist/communist belief that the means of production — and especially those of broad importance to the national well-being, such as energy production and distribution — should be managed for the common good. Why this usually led to state ownership rather than co-operative ownership is a subject of study in itself.

- The failure or near-failure of strategically important private sector businesses. In many cases the only rescuer available was the government of the day. Examples include Rolls-Royce in the United Kingdom, IRI in Italy, and many of Greece's nationalised companies. In most instances organisations remained in state ownership when they recovered, partly, at least, from inertia.

- The perceived need to pump-prime new areas of technology — examples include Amersham International and British Aerospace in the United Kingdom.

- The natural preference of public sector agencies to deal with their own kind. This led, inexorably, to the expansion in Britain of the activities carried out by local authorities through their own labour force, rather than through subcontractors — aided, in many cases, by political ideology.

It was inevitable that this process of creeping nationalisation would eventually create a backlash. By the late 1970s the word privatisation was in common usage in Britain, a usage that extended from the City to the man in the street. There were several forces at work to promote the concept of returning enterprises to the private sector. Research showed that state-owned companies were generally less efficient than their privately-owned counterparts and were often a drain on the country's resources. In Britain, privatisation was in line with the Thatcher government's policies of *laissez-faire* and popular capitalism. It also filled the country's coffers at a time when tax increases were not a politically viable option.

Britain led the race to unburden the state of its commercial trappings. It was rapidly followed by developing countries, such as Chile, and by much of Western Europe, including states such as France, which had socialist governments. More recently, we have seen the beginnings of privatisation across the countries of Eastern Europe, which are bent on returning the majority of industrial production and service sector organisations to private ownership.

2

Just as the nationalisation process had raised fierce debate and controversy, so the privatisation process has attracted both champions and critics.

The Arguments for Privatisation

As Colin Chapman points out in his book *Selling the Family Silver*: 'The British government may have been responsible for the start of the populist privatisation push, but it cannot take credit for establishing the word in the English vocabulary. As might be expected, it was an Americanism created by the management guru and author Professor Peter Drucker. Arguments for privatisation were outlined in his book, *The Age of Discontinuity: Guidelines to our Changing Society*, published in 1969. In it, Drucker says that the purpose of government is to govern — to design strategy and to make decisions. If government has to run business it is distracted from its fundamental task, which is to govern.'

Peter Lilley, appointed Britain's Financial Secretary in the autumn of 1989, put the Conservative government's view in a speech to Glasgow Business School, where he claimed that the prime benefits of privatisation were:

More efficient use of resources: Even when a monopoly cannot sensibly be broken up into competing companies, the incentives and disciplines of private enterprise and ownership are of immense value. The profit motive is a powerful spur both to satisfying customers and to the efficient use of resources.

Better protection for the consumer and the environment: The only way to ensure single-minded regulation is to ensure that regulation is the sole function of an independent regulator, leaving ownership to the private sector.

Wider share ownership: Privatisation has meant that there are more people owning shares in the companies whose products they use. . . . The fact that managers and employees can be, and usually are, shareholders too gives them a direct stake in the company's success . . . the coming water and electricity privatisations should develop share ownership still further by encouraging customers to buy shares in their own local water and electricity companies.

Overall, about half a million employees — 90 per cent of those eligible — have become shareholders in privatised companies. But we have also wanted to encourage individuals more generally to hold shares directly, rather than solely through savings institutions and pension funds.

Largely as a result of the major privatisation sales in which the general public were invited to invest, there are now nine million adult shareholders in the UK representing 20 per cent of the adult population, three times the number in 1979.

Sir Geoffrey Howe also made claims for the increased efficiency of private companies: 'a private firm must adapt its production — in quality, specification, cost and volume — to what the consumer will buy or go out of business. In the private sector the consumer is generally sovereign. In the public sector he is all too often dethroned by subsidy or monopoly.'

Nicholas Ridley, when British Trade Secretary, maintained: 'Achieving competition remains the key element in any privatisation.'

The World Bank has also espoused privatisation as a way of solving problems in the developing world, according to Colin Chapman, who explains:

Privatisation has become one of the favoured policies of the World Bank and the International Monetary Fund, as they seek to deal with the problem of Third World debt. Soft loans are now unfashionable as aid: the buzz word in Washington is now 'restructuring'. One form of reducing state spending and borrowing in this process of structural adjustment is to sell off state assets; many are assets in name only, because they have become state liabilities. Privatisation is one way a near bankrupt nation can attract overseas capital.

According to John Vickers and Vincent Wright in *The Politics of Privatisation in Western Europe*, the right wing in both France and Britain are in favour of denationalisation for strategic political reasons. They maintain that privatisation is a way of shifting the boundary between the public and the private in favour of the latter. They also claim that the motives for privatisers in Britain since 1983 and in France from 1986 to 1988 have been ideologically inspired and rooted in a wider strategy, whereas elsewhere they are more a reponse to pragmatic requirements. The authors point to the title of the French Minister of Finance's defence of his programme: *Je crois en l'homme plus qu'en l'État.* They explain: 'Self-help and self-reliance are the cardinal virtues, and they are being undermined by collective provision.'

One of the economic reasons for privatisation, according to Wright and Vickers, is that it facilitates the adoption of tough labour policies by distancing governments from unpalatable political choices: 'Private management, it is alleged, is more likely to tackle the unions which protect inefficient work practices and employment levels.' The authors also point out that some countries have privatised in the hope that it will widen capital markets by bringing in new investors, and deepen them by introducing mature companies with strong market positions. Supporters in Europe have also claimed that privatisation fosters the growth of the stock exchange.

In Spain and Italy, say the authors, the pragmatists who head up the rambling state holding companies, INI, IRI, and ENI, saw privatisation as a way of rationalising asset portfolios and reorganising investment strategies. Through privatisation, they could hive off loss-making or marginal operations, improve their balance sheets, and induce greater sensitivity to product specialisation. Privatisation would even facilitate the process of mergers, currently thought necessary to gain the size required by international competition and an increasingly integrated European market. The sale of SEAT to Volkswagen and Alfa Romeo to Fiat were justified in those terms. The argument about economies of scale was also cited in France when the privatised Compagnie Générale d'Électricité (CGE), the telecommunications and heavy-engineering group, merged its telecommunications assets with ITT in a joint venture, which created the world's second largest telecommunications group, after AT&T.

It is not just the privatised companies that have benefited, say the enthusiasts. Madsen Pirie, president of the Adam Smith Institute, declared in an article in *Capital Account Magazine*:

The impact of privatisation has been far larger than that which affected the companies themselves. They were indeed improved beyond the expectations of most observers; but the improvement affected other private industries through a beneficial effect on their inputs. With improved services, competitive pricing and alternative choices, other businesses have seen benefits to their own performance. Since privatisation affected so many inputs such as energy, transportation and communications, other firms have made gains to their own profitability as a result. They now have access to services which are more efficient, more responsive, cheaper and more varied than they were when the state ran them. Even the residual public sector has made gains. Services not yet privatised have improved their performances in the expectation that their turn will come. The process of preparing for entry into the private market has proved a salutary discipline. The privatisation programme has created a whole 'culture of privatisation' affecting even those still left in the public sector.

The Case Against Privatisation

Bill Callaghan, an official of the British Trades Union Congress, put the argument against privatisation cogently in an article for the magazine, *European Research* (August 1988):

(a) Privatisation is a doctrinaire policy which ignores evidence that public enterprise is a vital ingredient of modern economies — guaranteeing certain services and promoting the national interest in ways that the private sector cannot or will not.

(b) Privatisation in Britain is not expanding competition, as its supporters claimed it would — instead, it is sponsoring a series of massive private monopolies or near-monopolies.

(c) Again contrary to early claims, privatisation is not about rescuing state-owned loss makers and transforming them into profitability — all the public industries sold on the London Stock Exchange were profitable and successful before being privatised.

(d) The actual disposal of assets — typically via the Stock Exchange — has been grossly mishandled, with company after company being seriously undervalued on privatisation and then leaping to a premium that rewards speculators with quick profits. Total undervaluation is reckoned to be at least £3.6 billion. [N.B. This was before the water and electricity sell-off.]

(e) TUC research suggests that privatisation damages industrial relations, undermines job and income security, and makes it harder for unions to represent members effectively.

(f) Privatisation seems to be making life worse for consumers: the catalogue of poor performance by local service contractors has been a major factor in local and health authorities' refusal to privatise services on a big scale; while independent evidence suggests consumers are more dissatisfied with British Telecom now than before its sell-off.

Callaghan's co-author, Charles Isley of the survey organisation National Opinion Polls, also reports on a survey of public opinion on privatisation in the same magazine. The results, he maintains,

> . . . show that there was a solid majority of the public who continue to support the public ownership of essential services like water, electricity, gas; defence factories and naval dockyards; basic core industries and local bus services. It was the feeling that the industries that had been privatised by that time, the major one being British Telecom, had been sold too cheaply.

Britain's Labour Party has been strongly opposed to most of the privatisations and the manner in which they have been carried out. In some cases, water, for example, the party has a clear commitment to renationalisation. However, the party is at some pains not to commit itself to the enormous costs of direct and immediate renationalisation. It explained to *The Financial Times*: 'We accept that it will not be possible to take the industry into public ownership from day one, but powers in the Water Act would enable a Labour minister to alter the priorities of the existing regulatory regime.' These powers could include tightening regulatory control to the point where the private sector companies had relatively little freedom of decision-making, insisting that new targets for water quality are met in shorter timetables, and reducing the increases in charges to the extent that the privatised ventures would not be able to pay attractive dividends to their shareholders. As a politically acceptable solution, this may be far more attractive than raising taxes to reverse the sale of 'state silver'. But the solution only applies in practical terms to utilities and other monopolies or duopolies.

The number of small shareholders has risen dramatically in some countries as a result of privatisation. France, for example, has seen growth from 1 million to 5.5 million, and

Britain from 2 million to 9 million. But in practice, few of these people are more than one-time purchasers (indeed, more than half of all British shareholders own shares in only one company). Moreover, as Malcolm Bruce, the spokesman on privatisation for the UK's Liberal Democrats, has pointed out, the numbers tend to rise at a major flotation and gradually decline as people cash in their shares.

Chapman has stern words to say about the results of the British Airports Authority's post-privatisation policy, which he claims has led to overpricing and unnecessary diversification:

Of British Airports Authority's total revenue of £523 million in the 1987–88 year, less than half (43.6%) was accounted for by activities which directly related to the flying business. The lion's share (53.9%) came from duty-free shops, other retailing, and activities like car parking. Now that the BAA is trying to squeeze profit from every corner, it can cost more to park a car at Heathrow and Gatwick than in London's West End or City. Such is the disadvantage of having a government only too ready to hand out a private monopoly. . . . Whereas most airports are limited to a news stand, a gift shop and a duty-free shop on the air side of customs and immigration, the terminals at London's Heathrow Airport are like a *galleria* with branches of the Sock Shop, Tie Rack and Shirt Shop, and large supermarkets where you can buy everything from wine gums to waistcoats. Gatwick is even worse . . . . Most of this is the consequence of privatisation. The directors of the BAA seem to get as much joy from the tinkling of cash registers on the shopping parades as from the prompt departure of a flight.

Mexico has a large privatisation programme. Critics of the sell-off there claim that the government has *created* rather than broken monopolies with its programme. Cananea, a major copper company, was sold to Mexico's only other major copper company, which now has control of 96 per cent of the copper market. Others complain that Mexico's huge conglomerates have picked up too many of the firms. Some say that the government has been too generous to these large companies in return for support of its economic programme and price controls. In Mexico, commented Damian Fraser in *The Financial Times*, the government is probably too concerned with raising revenues and too unconcerned with the effect that privatisation is having on Mexico's industrial structure.

A Look to the Future

No doubt the arguments for and against privatisation will continue for some years, for even as the pace of privatisation slows down in the pioneer countries, such as Britain, it is quickening elsewhere. The determining factors will surely include:

- The strength of political ideology for and against the principle of privatisation;

- The level of confidence the government of the day has in its own ability to carry a programme through. It is noticeable that the Eastern bloc countries which are having the greatest difficulty in handling privatisation are those with the least stable governments — including the Soviet Union, where internal bickering within the government has paralysed moves towards a free market economy;

- The degree to which public and politicians will accept foreign ownership of major companies without imposing untenable restrictions;

- The degree to which banks and governments can agree on novel forms of financing, such as debt-for-equity swaps;

- The health of the financial sector, as a source of funding;

- The degree of patience governments can muster in preparing enterprises for sale — the programmes of several countries have been set back by disastrous experiences, caused by rushing enterprises into the private sector too early;

- The availability of good professional advice;

- The sheer capacity of local and global money markets to absorb a multitude of large flotations and acquisitions.

All the signs are that privatisation will be a significant factor in the global economy for at least the next decade. It is to be hoped that organisations which are privatised during that time will be able to learn from the good and bad experiences of those privatised in the 1990s. We hope that the cases in this book will povide some of those lessons.

Part I

PRIVATISATION AROUND THE WORLD

The motivation, mode, scope and experience of privatisation varies from country to country. Divestiture on the stock market is rare outside the developed world because of the lack of a well-functioning capital market and a substantial body of investors. Thus, Western-style privatisations have occurred in only a few countries, mainly Malaysia, Singapore and Korea. More commonly, the government sells back to the former owners those enterprises which it had taken over. Bangladesh, Chile and what was East Germany show examples of this. Management contracts and leasing are also a favoured method of the developing world. In this book we have endeavoured to capture case studies that illustrate a little of this diversity.

1

THE UNITED KINGDOM

The United Kingdom has led the privatisation boom. Firstly, it sold off companies which had come into state ownership through distress. Then, with confidence in the process, it sold off the major monopoly utilities such as water, electricity and telecommunications, and liberalised an increasing number of state agencies.

For state-owned enterprises there are several ways to become assimilated into the private sector:

Direct Sale

In such instances an organisation is sold directly to another company for an agreed price. This can given rise to claims that the price was unfair. For example, Girobank — the Post Office's bank — was sold to the Alliance and Leicester Building Society in mid-1990. The sale was one of the most drawn out, with the government taking ten months to agree a preferred purchaser and more than an additional year to organise the sale.

Buy-out

The National Freight Company was sold to the workforce, who pooled their savings and, in many cases, mortgaged their homes to buy shares. After four years their capital gain was about 1000 per cent.

Other cases have involved the complete break-up of the firm into many buy-outs, as occurred with the National Bus Company. British Steel, British Shipbuilders and BL/Austin Rover sold off parts to buy-out teams as part of a restructuring prior to privatisation.

Buy-outs have generally been one of the most successful forms of divestment because the workforce, who have in-depth knowledge of the company, now have the incentive to make it more efficient. Vickers Shipbuilding and Engineering Ltd, another successful employee buy-out, is described in some detail on pages 141 to 147.

The National Bus Company was sold as seventy separate regional operating subsidiaries. Some were sold to private sector companies, but the majority (forty) to their managers and employees. Competition was encouraged by licensing new carriers as well.

However, there have been charges that, in some cases, buy-out managers have bought businesses too cheaply. The concerns registered by the Investment Committee of the National Association of Pension Funds and by the Institutional Shareholders Committee refer to all management buy-outs, and cover, among other things, the very different level of information about the business and its prospects which is available to the management, compared to that available to other would-be purchasers. The question arises, whether the managers of the enterprise should be using their offices to obtain the best price for their shareholders or for themselves.

Table 1.1   Public sector buy-outs in the United Kingdom to April 1989

Source	Number of buy-outs
British Aerospace	1
BL/Austin Rover	14
British Rail	6
British Shipbuilders	9
British Steel	10
BTG/NEB	12
National Bus	39
National Freight	1
Local authority services	6
Other buy-outs	4
Buy-ins	10
TOTAL:	112

(Source: CMBOR (Centre for Management Buy-out Research) — an independent research centre founded by Spicer and Oppenheimer and Barclays Development Capital at the University of Nottingham)

Competitive Tendering for Local Authority and National Health Service Activities

The big shake-up here came in 1988 with the Local Government Act. This required councils to invite bids from both private companies and their own staff direct-service organisations to run seven services: school meals, other catering, refuse collection, street cleaning, building cleaning, grounds maintenance and vehicle maintenance. Subsequently other services such as sports field maintenance and leisure services were added, and yet others could follow, such as legal, architect and computer services. Councils are now unable to award their own works department a contract without first proving that the bid was commercially realistic and that the terms of the tender were not anti-competitive.

The policy has not always opened up town hall services to outside contractors. In many areas the council's direct service organisations have kept their former monopolies virtually intact, winning about 80 per cent of contracts put out to tender. Evidence shows that the first round of tendering has more impact on the organisation and business practices of local authorities than on the provision of services themselves.

Agency Status

The government implemented a programme in 1991 to hand over the work of government departments to semi-autonomous agencies. By the end of April, 50 such agencies, employing 200,000 civil servants, were operating.

Privatisation by Flotation

Flotations had raised £29 billion prior to the privatisation of water and electricity, with most of the flotations successful in the sense that they were oversubscribed. Today some of Britain's largest and most profitable companies are businesses that were previously state owned. Major institutions and individuals all took a share in the country's industry, although the volume of small shareholders fell off rapidly — in most cases they cashed in their shares. One of the few flops was the Britoil sale, where the price was too high to attract investors.

Table 1.2 below shows the privatisations by flotation in chronological order:

Table 1.2 Privatisation flotations in the United Kingdom to April 1991

Enterprise	Date of privatisation	Sum raised (£bn)	Issue price (£)
Cable & Wireless	Nov 1981	0.9	2.93
Amersham International	Feb 1982	0.1	1.42
Associated British Ports	Apr 1984	0.1	1.12
Enterprise Oil	Jun 1984	0.4	1.85
Jaguar	Jul 1984	0.3	1.65
British Telecom	Nov 1984	3.9	1.30
British Aerospace	May 1985	0.6	3.75
Britoil	Aug 1985	0.5	1.85
British Gas	Dec 1986	5.4	1.35
British Airways	Feb 1987	0.9	1.25
Rolls-Royce	May 1987	1.4	1.70
British Airports Authority	Jul 1987	1.3	2.45
British Petroleum	Oct 1987	7.0	3.30
British Steel	Dec 1988	2.5	1.25
Water Companies	Nov 1989	5.3	2.40
Electricity Distribution Companies	Dec 1990	8.0	2.40
Electricity Generating Companies	Mar 1991	2.0	1.75

From an investor's point of view, most of the privatisations have been successful. Some have shown significant gains in share value — most notably Jaguar, where the share price had risen by 4.5 times before it was taken over by Ford. Others, such as BP and British Steel, have stagnated in value. Most issues have been oversubscribed, allowing investors to reap an immediate profit by selling on the first day of trading. Financial Secretary Peter Lilley said in 1989:

> After eight years of profit growth since privatisation, Cable and Wireless have increased their profits six-fold since privatisation. The profits of Associated British Ports are up eight-fold. Enterprise Oil [the former oil interest of the nationalised British Gas corporation] have doubled their proven reserves of oil and gas — the central assets of any oil exploration and production company — during last year alone. British Airways have reported passenger and cargo loads at records levels and have received a number of awards during the year for the high levels of customer service provided for their passengers.

Four of the privatised enterprises now rank among the top twenty most profitable companies in Britain — British Telecom, with pre-tax profits in 1989 of £2.4 billion, in fact ranked top.

The pace of issues has been governed by a number of factors, both political and market related. The political will to privatise did not always take full account of the practical difficulties — Royal Ordnance, for example, ran the full gamut of privatisation options before it was finally sold to British Aerospace as a going concern. Depressed market conditions after the 1987 stock market crash made flotation less attractive for a considerable period afterwards. At other times, the sheer scale of investment required would have distorted the capital markets, starving other companies of investment and driving prices down generally, so it was necessary to stagger the really big sell-offs to allow the market to cope. Even before water privatisation, the newly privatised companies accounted for around a sixth of the entire capitalisation of the London stock market, or about £60 billion.

It is worth looking briefly at some of these sell-offs.

Amersham International

Amersham International was formerly the radioisotope-handling subsidiary of the United Kingdom Atomic Energy Authority. Involved in radioactive materials packaging and medical equipment, it was profitable and successful before its privatisation in February 1982. The share offer was over-subscribed twenty-four times. The number of small share-holders fell within one month from 62 000 to 10 000 as small buyers made a quick killing by selling to big investors. After initial strong performance financially, Amersham has tended to underperform in the market in recent years, although it still has a share price more than double the issue price.

Associated British Ports

Formerly the British Transport Docks Board, set up by the 1963 Transport Act, it operates nineteen ports including Southampton, Hull, Grimsby and Immingham.

The organisation, which was sold in two parts, was profit-able before the sell-off. First, 51.5 per cent of the government's stake was sold for £46 million in 1983. The remainder was sold off in April 1984. The income from the first sale was offset by the fact that the government agreed to cancel ABP's outstanding debt of £81.3 million.

The 1983 sell-off was oversubscribed thirty-five times. The shares, which were initially offered for 112p, rose to 145p within one month. This led to charges of undervaluing. The issue included a free share offer to employees, who ended up with just under 5 per cent of the shares after the sale. Although

19.6 million shares were sold to the public, by December 1983 a mere thirty-three holdings accounted for 59 per cent of the equity not held by employees or government. Significantly, by 1984 the share price had doubled and the remaining shares were floated at 250p per share.

Enterprise Oil

Enterprise Oil was created from the oil exploration assets held by British Gas. It had an estimated asset value of £540 million and huge potential profitability. The government sold all but a golden share in June 1984 for £392 million.

The shares were offered at 185p, but despite the offer of a discount they were undersubscribed. Mining multinational Rio Tinto Zinc (RTZ) bid for 49 per cent of the shares and had to be blocked by the government. It was restricted to a 10 per cent stake, but later managed to acquire a further 19.9 per cent interest. *The Financial Times*, on 26 June 1984, described the RTZ affair as 'a catastrophic conclusion to what was already one of the most blighted privatisation ventures'. The employee holding of Enterprise Oil was just 0.03 per cent of the share capital.

In 1989, Enterprise Oil made profits of £288 500 per employee and paid its 234 staff an average of £32 000 per annum, making it one of Britain's most profitable companies.

Jaguar

Jaguar represents one of the best examples of how a company freed from the restrictions of a state-owned parent, in this case British Leyland, can revitalise its operations. It is probably true to say, however, that if BL had been a private sector company, it would have behaved in much the same way towards Jaguar — the entire organisation had been stratified and bureaucratised to a high degree.

The sell-off produced a near-riot in the City in July 1984 as would-be buyers rushed to purchase the shares, which were widely believed to have been undervalued. The share issue was oversubscribed 8.3 times. Shares were offered at 165p each and rose to 179p on the same day. Less than one in five Jaguar workers opted to become share-owners, and they ended up with just 1.3 per cent of the shares. According to the *Investors Chronicle* (11 January 1985), six months after the sale, many shareholders had sold out and only 50 000 remained from an initial 120 000.

In the medium term, Jaguar was not big enough to survive on its own, and its sale to a larger organisation was inevitable in retrospect.

British Telecom

British Telecom's story is told in greater detail on pages 91 to 110. Like British Airways, which also has its own chapter in this book, BT had to make radical transformations in the way it perceived and dealt with its customers. But by March 1990, the effort had paid off and it emerged as Britain's most profitable company with pre-tax profits of over £2 billion.

British Aerospace

British Aerospace, another of our case studies, came together as a nationalised industry through the 1977 Aircraft and Shipbuilding Industries Act. The British Aerospace Act 1980 formed the corporation into a public company owned by the secretary of state. The government sold a 51.6 per cent stake for £148.6 million in February 1981. Offsetting the £148.6 million sell-off price were a number of factors. Firstly, there were over £5 million sell-off expenses, then £100 million payment to BAe for new shares subscribed, and finally £55 million worth of dividends.

There was an 83 per cent drop in the number of BAe shareholders within less than a year. The number of small shareholders who held less than 100 shares plummeted from 44 000 to 3 300, and by the end of 1983 197 shareholders owned three-quarters of the shares. The remaining government stake in the company was sold in the mid-1980s, with the government retaining a golden share. British Aerospace is particularly interesting because it has subsequently taken over other large enterprises, privatised by direct sale.

British Airways

The British Airways story is told on pages 127 to 140. BA is interesting for a number of reasons. Firstly, because of the scale of the culture change that had to be undergone to prepare it for privatisation — BA had to rebuild a customer orientation that had been lost in its years as a state-owned enterprise. Secondly, because of the scale of its ambitions. Once it had achieved its position as one of the most successful and profitable airlines in the world, BA in recent years has concentrated much of its efforts on developing international alliances and part ownerships of other countries' carriers, under a strategy aimed at making it one of potentially only two or three truly global carriers.

Britoil

Britoil was the oil production and exploration part of the British National Oil Corporation (BNOC), the public organisation set up by Labour's Petroleum and Submarine Pipelines Act in 1975. Britoil was split away from BNOC in 1982, and

BNOC itself was later abolished. The government's stake was sold through two flotations. The first part of the sell-off in 1982 raised over £548 million before expenses.

BP

BP was Britain's largest industrial company with a majority public stake until 1979. The government sold 5 per cent of BP for £276 million in October 1979. In 1983, it reduced its stake to 39 per cent by selling shares to the value of a further £565 million. The 1979 sale offered shares at 363p. These immediately rose in price. The 1983 sale offered shares at 435p each. In the following year they sold for 540p.

By March 1990, BP held thirteenth place in a table of Britain's most profitable companies, with profits per employee of over £16,000. However, a BP flotation was responsible for the privatisation banana skin that most people remember. This was the fourth tranche of BP shares, and was launched in the aftermath of the October 1987 stock market crash. The government was bailed out by the Kuwait Investment Office, which mopped up the shares.

Cable and Wireless

Cable and Wireless (see pages 187 to 200) provides telecommunications services and facilities and has extensive overseas operations. By 1983 the government had sold the majority of the profitable company in two tranches. Its remaining 23 per cent stake was sold at a later date. The 1981 sale was oversubscribed five times. In this flotation, shareholders who bought shares at 168p on day one could sell them two months later at 210p.

National Freight Consortium

Previously the National Freight Company, it owned British Road Services, National Carriers, Roadline UK, Pickfords and other freight concerns. In the run-up to its sell-off, the government turned NFC into a limited liability company through the Transport Act of 1980. The company was sold to a consortium of managers and employees in February 1982 for £53.5 million. The shares in NFC were initially offered at 25p each, and many employees remortgaged their houses to buy a stake in their business.

Sealink

This former ferry and harbour subsidiary of British Rail had a 1983 fleet of thirty-eight ships and another fifteen owned in partnership with overseas ferry firms, plus assets of over £100 million. The Bermuda-registered company, British Ferries, bought Sealink for £65.7 million in 1984. The government retains a golden share to be exercised in the interests of national defence.

Water

Among the most ambitious privatisations for the government was that of the ten water authorities in England and Wales. At the outbreak of the Second World War there were some two thousand enterprises — both private companies and local authorities — supplying water in the two countries. A series of Acts of Parliament had reduced these by 1973 to ten large regional water authorities and twenty-nine statutory water companies. The latter retained their independence. The idea behind the 1973 reforms was to bring all aspects of water management within each river basin under the control of the same authority, from water supply through sewage treatment and pollution control to leisure activities such as fishing.

At first, water was one of the least likely targets for privatisation. Although there were clearly significant problems arising from conflict of interest between the various responsibilities of the authorities, water was a low-profile activity. Moreover, the industry had suffered from years of inadequate capital expenditure, making it relatively unattractive to the private investor.

Several things happened to change that perspective. Firstly, management changes in the water authorities replaced the large, unwieldy boards made up of local council representatives with smaller, professional executive boards. At the same time, increasing criticism of water quality, both at home and from the European Community (eventually to lead to prosecutions in the European Court) put the industry into the limelight and obliged the government to allow increases in capital expenditure.

Matters came to the boil in 1985, however, when the chairman of Thames Water, one of the largest authorities, refused to repay £40 million to the Treasury (an act that would have increased consumers' bills by 10 per cent) unless told to by the House of Commons. Although the government majority made the House's decision a foregone conclusion, enough Conservative MPs voted against or abstained to bring the issue of water well and truly into the limelight.

Thames Water took the initiative and asked to be privatised, stimulating debate on an issue that was now already on ministers' tables. The idea evoked fierce opposition from organisations such as the Confederation of British Industry, which was concerned (paradoxically) at the possibility of exploitation by private companies. The scale of the opposition forced the Department of the Environment to back down. A year later, however, the Conservative Party manifesto promised to set up a National Rivers Authority to regulate the industry, while the authorities themselves would be privatised. This time it was the water industry itself that raised an outcry, on the grounds that the river basin concept would be undermined. But the government insisted that the new regulatory body was part of the price of privatisation and eventually, with great reluctance, all ten authorities agreed.

Meanwhile, several French water companies had made raids to acquire substantial shareholdings in several of the statutory water authorities. Opponents of water privatisation were able to point to the spectre of foreign ownership of a vital resource.

The flotation plans next ran into problems over how to ensure the new companies did not increase water prices excessively after privatisation. To a certain extent the NRA would do this, and would ensure that they met standards of water quality and pollution control. But the water authorities needed to continue and increase the pace of capital investment, particularly if they were to meet the directives from the European Community. Government negotiators agreed with each authority separately how much it would increase charges each year, in a series of discussions that led to several threats of resignation.

At the same time, a concerted campaign by the Labour opposition emphasised the problems the newly-privatised companies would face and the environmental damage that might result from returning the resources to private hands. The land surrounding reservoirs in National Parks would no longer be protected, they argued. Moreover, the need to create profits for a large number of shareholders would either raise charges even further, or reduce the amount spent on critical improvements to the treatment and delivery systems. To keep the flotation on course, the government had eventually to agree to write off £5 billion of debt and to inject a further £1.6 billion.

Given its complexity (the ten authorities were all very different in background, profile, net worth and attractiveness as investments), the amount of investment cash required, and the scale of opposition, the flotation could easily have left the government with egg on its face. In the event, the sell-off was oversubscribed.

Electricity

The saga of the sale of the twelve regional electricity distribution companies, PowerGen, and National Power has been a succession of blunders and revised plans.

One of the more dramatic features of the electricity privatisation was the disagreement between the minister responsible for initiating it and the head of the Central Electricity Generating Board, Lord Marshall of Goring. Marshall had planned for the CEGB to be privatised as an on-going monopoly, as had been the case with British Gas. But the Energy Secretary, Cecil Parkinson, had been convinced that there would be a political outcry if he attempted to do the same thing with electricity. Marshall was given chairmanship of National Power, the larger of the two generating companies to be formed and privatised out of the CEGB.

The public debate brought under scrutiny by the House of Commons Energy Committee a great deal of previously secret data about the real costs of generating electricity. These revealed that, contrary to claims by various administrations over the years, nuclear energy was not a low-cost alternative, and that the inclusion of the older nuclear power plants within the privatised enterprises would involve massive public subsidies. The government had little choice but to withdraw these nuclear power stations from the sale. Lord Marshall, the leading champion of nuclear power, resigned.

The initial intention to sell off the two electricity generating operations was by flotation. But the uncertain state of the stock market made a straightforward sale more attractive in the short term. A free-for-all developed in which a variety of candidates bid for the smaller of the two organisations, PowerGen. The government favoured a direct sell to Hanson Industries. Hanson reportedly demanded a £15 million cash payment to cover its bid and other costs, but this caused such an outcry that the government had to declare it would not countenance 'sweeteners'. Hanson's offer stimulated a bid from the Union of Democratic Mineworkers (the smaller union, not affiliated to

29

the Trades Union Congress, representing workers in the coal industry, PowerGen's main suppliers) together with City interests. It also brought into the open proposals for a management buy-out, in which management and employees would receive 10 per cent of the equity, two industrial partners would receive 35 per cent, and the rest would be held by City institutions. Interest was also reported from earlier privatisations, such as British Gas and BP, and from traditionally private sector companies such as GEC.

Additional complications arose. For example, the unions in the electricity supply side of the business issued a demand for free share allocations of £2000 to all staff, and generous concessions on bonus shares to staff who subscribed to the flotation offer. A precedent was established with water privatisation, where employees were given £70 worth of shares.

National Power's preparations for privatisation have included a massive £914 million write-off on its 1990 accounts, to cover 6000 job losses (out of a total employee headcount of 22 000) and the shutting down of various obsolete coal-powered generating plants. The costs of preparing for privatisation itself have been put by the company at £80 million.

British viewers were treated to a marketing campaign for the power sell-off throughout the autumn of 1990. Potential investors were asked to register their interest with a share information office. Pre-registration provides an initial list of names and addresses which simplifies administration in complex flotations like water and electricity.

Electricity companies were saddled with borrowings as they entered the private sector, and it has yet to be seen what effect this will have on their financial performance. The electricity distributors were sold off in late 1990, while the sale of the electricity generators, PowerGen, National Power and the Scottish companies finally took place by flotation in early 1991.

Local Authority Privatisations

Privatisation in local government has taken two main forms: the direct placement of work, previously carried out by retained labour, with independent, private sector companies; and the creation of private companies by local authority employees, which subcontract to do the same work as before.

The overall move to subcontract local authority services has been politically inspired rather than the result of efficiency planning — hence the much greater take-up of opportunities by Conservative-led councils. However, the protagonists for this kind of privatisation argue that contracting out increases efficiency in a number of ways:

- operational cost savings, particularly from a reduced head-count, but also because it is easier to control expenditure via an external contractor working to a fixed-price contract;

- improved service;

- more motivated staff.

Opponents of the process dispute all these. On the financial side, for example, while some local authorities report considerable success, others have evoked considerable controversy. For example, West Wiltshire District Council received strong criticism from a government-appointed auditor for its handling of the linked subcontracting of an operation to sell computer software to other local authorities. The department concerned had developed innovative programmes to handle tasks such as the new community charge. In July 1988, when some thirty councils had signed up as customers for the new software, the department managers set up West Wiltshire Information Systems, a private company, which spun off the operation under a deal in which profits were divided between the new company and the council. The Labour Party claimed the deal would cost taxpayers in Wiltshire £20 million over five years. Another local authority was criticised by the auditor for an agreement to allow its solicitors to privatise themselves, in a deal that cost the council £75 000 a year more than when they did the same job in house.

There have also been a number of cases where service has quite clearly deteriorated. Moreover, the argument over whether motivation is improved is still unresolved — certainly there can be short-term problems in motivating those whose jobs are not privatised.

Those local authority privatisations that have taken place through the management buy-out route often require additional skills to be brought in to make them viable businesses. In particular, they may need strong finance directors to provide the financial controls and disciplines that would previously have been exerted centrally.

The UK National Audit Office registered particular concern at the manner in which buy-outs were handled at several new town corporations. It found that three corporations, where staff had been allowed to set up separate companies to bid for the service they used to provide in house, had altogether seen eight hundred staff leave to go to thirty-seven such ventures. These enterprises won contracts worth £37 million. Two of the three corporations paid out £6.6 million in redundancy awards to staff, who continued to do the same job but through an intermediary employer. Moreover, many of the contracts were won without competitive tendering. The lesson appears to be that stricter controls need to be instituted at the early, planning stages of such buy-outs.

Further Privatisations

Although most of the obvious candidates for privatisation have already been moved wholly or partly into the private sector, there still remain a number of significant options. Among them:

Prisons

The government has studied with interest the experience of several states in the USA which have permitted private sector companies to take over the administration of prisons for non-violent criminals and young offenders.

Coal

The privatisation of electricity will have a significant impact upon British Coal. In years past, the CEGB was persuaded to accept more coal-fired plants than it would have preferred, in order to maintain jobs in the coal industry. The CEGB did not suffer, because it could pass on the costs to the consumers — a long-standing complaint of British manufacturing industry.

Under the new regime, however, National Power and PowerGen have no such obligations beyond the first three years. Moreover, the cost of operating coal-fired stations is rising as EEC regulations demand the fitting of expensive desulphurisation equipment to reduce pollution. Both power generating companies now intend to focus investment on new gas-fired plants. Where they continue to use coal-fired stations, they will increasingly use imported, low-sulphur coal.

Although the government has made no announcements regarding coal privatisation, the continuing decline in the industry makes it more and more of an albatross. The key question may be whether a sufficiently attractive package can be put together to persuade investors to buy. The European Commission has already quizzed the British Government over plans to write off accumulated debts and liabilities of over £6 billion in preparation for privatisation.

British Rail

Gradual reductions in government subsidy and increases in fares have been seen by many observers as preparation for privatisation. The fact that most countries' railways are still heavily subsidised makes BR a less attractive privatisation candidate, as does the lack of investment in many parts of the system. However, BR does have significant reserves of land, which would increase its asset value. It could also hive off profitable parts of the railway, or increase private sector involvement in its running.

InterCity and bulk freight might be viable by the mid-1990s, but Network SouthEast and the rest of the freight business are unlikely to prove sufficiently profitable before the end of the decade. The provincial passenger sector will always make losses. Sale of the entire railway system would also raise only modest proceeds. Although the business is worth between £10 billion and £15 billion, purchasers would be more concerned with earning potential than asset values, particularly if any strings were attached. The claimed benefits of privatisation would include a radical change in culture among BR managers and staff, greater flexibility over fares and pay, access to private capital for investment, and a closer relationship between customers and suppliers.

The Fire Service

The Adam Smith Institute, a champion of privatisation, has suggested that the fire service should be added to the six service areas that county and city councils already have to put out to tender. The institute claims that the fire service in England is one of the most expensive in the world, and points to experience in the USA and Denmark, where private sector fire services already operate.

The probation service

Government proposals released in early 1990 do not envisage the privatisation of the probation service as a whole, but do suggest that putting out much of the work to private sector organisations would 'help the objectives of protecting the public, reducing offending and securing value for money'.

British Technology Group

This is an agency under the Department of Trade and Industry, dealing with the licensing of British inventions. Top management is reported to be keen to privatise, particularly now that all the major litigation cases it had brought against overseas companies for patent infringement (for example, US defence contractors, which had used the technology behind the hovercraft without a licence) have been settled.

National Engineering Laboratory

Transferred into the ownership of a new company, National Technology Centre Ltd, in May 1989, after a report by accountants Touche Ross, it has already been the subject of one abortive sale bid.

Scottish Transport Group

This organisation is to be sold off as eleven job lots, based on its main operating divisions. These include the Scottish Bus Company, a ferry operation to the Western Isles, and subsidiaries in vehicle engineering, insurance, property and travel.

The canal system

The canal system currently costs £45 million a year in state subsidies. However, it has a huge portfolio of property, much of it undeveloped and in city centre sites, worth well over £1 billion. Two main options are under consideration for the

2000-mile network: either it will be sold as a going concern, once development plans for the properties have wiped out the need for subsidies, or the properties alone will be sold.

Marketing of a Flotation

The British have become experts at marketing mass flotations. PR agency Dewe Rogerson developed a basically similar approach to marketing British Telecom, water and electricity. Tony Carlisle, the chief executive, explained how it was done in the case of British Telecom to the *Director* magazine in April 1990: 'Our objective is to create a perception of scarcity. This is essential to flotation marketing. The whole definition of flotation success is to create more demand than there is a supply of shares.' He adds: 'The perception of scarcity was our marketing objective. A share offer is only successful if you have more demand than supply.'

The campaign's task was to convince individuals that they wanted to buy shares. Before the privatisation flotations, there were only two traditional sources of demand for shares: City institutions and overseas capital markets. The City could not oversubscribe an offer the size of British Telecom, and there was a limit to how much could be allowed to go abroad.

Dewe Rogerson commissioned an opinion poll which revealed that, out of 2000 people, 25 per cent would be interested in owning a share in the telecommunications company. He says: 'We said forget the 75 per cent, we don't need 10 million shareholders. This was the second principle of flotation marketing. Flotation marketing is converting interest, not creating interest.'

In April 1984, the company aimed to elicit two million enquiries and one million applications with the campaign. This was considered by some to be an impossible task, but for British Telecom, there were 1.4 million applications. Ministers and officials had been staggered by the £13 million budget earmarked for marketing. According to Mihir Bose of the *Director* magazine: 'Dewe Rogerson had created the marketing circle. First, make people think there is a scarcity, then use marketing and saturation advertising to make sure there is such a demand that a scarcity will be created.'

Catalogue of Problems

One of the major contentious issues in some of the largest privatisations has been that of regulation. Because British Gas and British Telecom, for example, remain effective monopolies, it has been essential to regulate their activities. In particular, the regulatory bodies set up to monitor the privatised utilities have focused on profit levels, quality of service and equity of service (British Telecom would have had good commercial reasons for downgrading its service to rural communities, for example, but Oftel is required to ensure that this does not happen). In practice, the regulatory regime is far less intrusive in commercial terms and far less bureaucratic than in the United States, which has the only other similar system in the developed world. Although there has not been sufficient time to evaluate the long-term impact on the consumer, the regular negotiations between the privatised utilities and their regulators have so far been relatively genteel.

Water is privately owned or operated in the USA and France and in some parts of the United Kingdom, and electricity distribution in the USA and Germany. So privatising utilities is not in itself new. What is new is the creation in Great Britain, where competition is either permanently or temporarily impracticable, of tough and clear regulatory regimes in order to give proper protection to customers.

Potentially more problematic is the issue of competition for these monopoly utilities. The balance between the privatised company's duty to use its resources to provide the best return for its shareholders, and the regulatory requirement to open up its networks for competitors to use, has already generated fierce arguments. These can be expected to become more frequent as the small number of competitors grows to the point where there is no longer a monopoly in practical terms. British Telecom, for example, is legally obliged to carry competitors' traffic.

The discussion continues — early in 1991, British Gas offered to surrender 10 per cent of the British industrial gas market to competitors by releasing back to suppliers 150 million cubic feet a day. According to competitors, the move, without precedent among Britain's privatised utilities, would disadvantage them because they do not own their own gas supplies.

The Future

In a recent survey of privatised companies by management consultants United Research, it was found that most have cut their labour force, sold peripheral businesses, and reorganised their activities to create profit centres. However, the survey concludes that, apart from BA and British Steel, who were forced to operate in commercial markets, few have created a fully commercial culture, especially among middle management. These managers were given a helping hand by the strong growth of the British economy in the mid-1980s. Now certain privatised companies are being forced to streamline their management, which is likely to lead to over 30 000 job losses in the economic downturn of the early 1990s.

2

CONTINENTAL EUROPE

Austria

Nationalisation of manufacturing industry in Austria came about, not for ideological reasons, but as a device for keeping enterprises in Austrian ownership at the end of the Second World War. There was a real danger at that time that companies might have been regarded as German property and therefore available for confiscation. Once manufacturing had been nationalised, however, the Social Democrats decided for ideological reasons that it should remain so and the conservative People's Party was content to maintain the *status quo.*

The impetus for privatisation came through disastrous performances and extensive mismanagement in several of these enterprises. However, this was also coupled with a desire to keep industry in Austrian hands, which is a major reason why moves towards privatisation have been so tentative. Some 40 per cent of Austrian industry is currently owned by overseas investors, such as BMW, Phillips and Chrysler. Even if xenophobia were not a factor, the Austrian bourse is simply too small to cope with a series of major flotations. So the Austrian government has slowly but surely released minority shareholdings to the market in companies such as Austrian Airlines, in the electricity supply industry or Verbund, in oil company OeMV (part of the industrial conglomerate Austrian

Industries), and in two major banks, Creditanstalt-Bankverein and Laenderbank.

As yet, however, there is little sign that the state will reduce its ownership to less than 50 per cent, and many of the most troubled enterprises — for example, engineering and steel company Voest-Alpine, another subsidiary of Austrian Industries, which made heavy losses in recent years — are not yet up for sale.

Belgium

Although Belgium's public sector accounted for nearly 60 per cent of gross national product in 1987 and, according to the magazine *International Management*, employed 11 per cent of the total population — perhaps the highest percentage outside the communist world — it has not gone far with its privatisation programme.

Belgium's state-owned investment company, Société Nationale d'Investissement (SNI), has been partially privatised through a share issue into a new holding company, Sofinim, which holds equity both in a variety of major Belgian companies, including airline Sabena and Channel Tunnel participants Belgamanche, and in a multiplicity of small companies. However, the shares are non-voting preference shares, so the control of the holding company and its assets remains with Société Nationale d'Investissement and therefore with the government.

An attempt to privatise Brussels' Zaventem Airport, with a sale by flotation of two-thirds of its equity, was postponed as a result of the stock exchange crash of 1987. Since then enthusiasm for the privatisation has waned and it remains in state hands.

Denmark

The government's biggest privatisation deal to date is the sale of the state life insurance company, Statsanstalten, to Baltica Insurance, the insurance arm of the Baltic financial services group. The sell-off, which brought in DKr3.4 billion (£570 million), has been hedged about by conditions which prevent the new owner from using profits which should be allocated to the policyholders. In addition, there will be a courtroom sequel to the deal. Two Socialist opposition members are suing the government on the grounds that the sale of the company is unconstitutional. They claim that the company belongs to the policyholders and is therefore not the state's to sell. (Source: Hilary Barnes, *The Financial Times*, 'Government sells Danish insurer', 2 October 1990.)

France

France announced its privatisation programme in the summer of 1986, following the election of a Conservative government. The programme privatised over sixty state enterprises, including banks and insurance groups. The glass-maker, Saint Gobain, the Paribas banking group and the Assurances Générales de France were some of the first to be denationalised. By October 1987 over half of the big state banks had been sold, including Groupe Financière de Suez (see pages 149 to 152). The French followed the British example and set up employee share-option schemes. Like the British, the French government retained a golden share in strategic industries and only allowed a set percentage to be sold abroad.

The first privatisations before the stock market slide of 1987 created 5 million new shareholders, with as much as 80 per cent of the workforces buying a share in their company. In this period, the French also took to buy-outs as an efficient method of transferring ownership. Managers have bought one whole state firm, IDI, but in general buy-outs have been divestments of peripheral activities from larger groups.

Table 2.1   French privatisation buy-outs to 1988

Buy-out	Vendor	Date
E&E Kay (UK)	Pechiney	1982
Constructions Chalonnaises	IDI	1984
Ultrasons Annemasse	Rhône Poulenc	1985
Docks Industriels	Pechiney	1985
Montupet	Pechiney	1986
Manurhin	Matra	1986
Institut Développement Ind	IDI	1987
Cameca	Thompson	1987
GSI	CGE	1987
OTH	Paribas	1987
Sidel	Saint Gobain	1987
Godde Bedin	Rhône Poulenc	1987
Profroid	Thompson	1987
Davum Commerce	Sacilor	1987
MECI	Elf Aquitaine	1988
Lebranchu	Matra	1988

(Source: CMBOR, Centre for Management Buy-out Research, University of Nottingham.)

Between these hectic few years and until April 1990, with some exceptions, Mitterand allowed neither privatisations nor nationalisations. The policy was criticised for curbing the freedom of state companies to form foreign partnerships and raise cash from private investors at a time when they had been trying to fund a wave of international takeovers. The change allows partial privatisation by letting domestic or foreign private groups take minority stakes of up to 49.9 per cent in state companies, on condition that they provide new capital for the state partner and form an industrial, commercial or financial co-operation accord.

One of the big exceptions was Renault, the state-owned car maker. Renault is making progress towards becoming a normal commercial company. It changed its status from a state-guaranteed *régie* in 1990 and it now has a share exchange accord with Volvo, the Swedish car group.

In general, the state sector still embraces public transport, telecommunications and energy utilities, plus the leading companies in aerospace and air transport, electronics, arms, banking, insurance, oil, gas, chemicals, tobacco and cars.

Greece

The Greek Government unveiled its privatisation plans in June 1990. Twenty-four heavily indebted state-owned indus-trial companies, all of which belong to the Industrial Recons-truction Organisation (IRO), will be put up for offer, either by flotation or direct sale. Greece has its own peculiar problems, since the state acquired many almost bankrupt companies during the Socialist's reign in the mid-seventies. These com-panies had often been nationalised voluntarily and were draining government resources.

Greek law had unintentionally encouraged this mass nation-alisation by maintaining that bankrupts were liable to criminal proceedings. So the Greek government acquired a motley band of enterprises that included breweries, restaurants, hotels and plastics factories. As for the others, often owned by some of Greece's wealthiest families, the government merely took over their debts, claiming that the production of everything from cement to textiles was of strategic importance. Since in most cases the debts largely outstripped the assets, the government immediately became a majority shareholder.

Yanos Gramatides Associates, one of the few Greek law firms with the international expertise necessary, were special advisors to the Greek government at the beginning of the denationalisation process. Gramatides himself has studied the British privatisations in detail and he has some harsh words to say about the Greek efforts. 'Some of these companies were previously owned by Greece's top families. They will not stand unprotestingly by if the government then sells off their former company for a large profit.'

The first five to be sold will include Minon, a major supermarket chain, but Gramatides has misgivings: 'The government only took over in April 1990 and wants to privatise as soon as possible. Its main criterion is speed. It has forgotten about marketing the company to potential shareholders, or investing resources and recruiting a new capable management team to sell it as an ongoing concern.' He warns: 'These industries need at least three years to build themselves up.'

Gramatides added: 'The government should not let urgency dictate its behaviour or it will do everyone an injustice by selling the companies well below their real price.' However, IRO's president, George Yannopoulos, hopes to sell off most of the companies by the end of 1991.

Opposed to the plan are the Greek trade unions and many of the employees of IRO companies. Some 30 000 went on strike to protest against the change of ownership and to support an alternative proposal from the Greek Industrialists Federation, under which the private sector would *lease* IRO companies for a period. Unlike the British or the French, the Greek government has not created any incentives for state employees to buy a share in their destiny.

Greece can expect a second wave of privatisation when the National Bank of Greece, which also owns a range of companies, decides to offload them.

Italy

In Italy, there are no set procedures for privatisation. The situation differs in each of the big state holding companies: IRI, ENI, EFIM. IRI needs no authorisation when it wants to sell an interest, ENI requires an authorisation if it involves the loss of control of the company, and EFIM must obtain permission, whatever the conditions of sale.

Between 1982 and 1987 IRI sold twenty-one companies and reduced its stake in others, cutting its workforce by 50 000 and netting 7 billion lire. In 1986, Fiat bought Alfa Romeo from IRI, setting a precedent for transferring a major industrial firm from the public to the private sector.

However, according to *The Financial Times* in November 1990, the Italian privatisation drive has floundered because:

- The political class is reluctant to surrender controls over sectors which account for more than a third of economic activity;
- the public holding companies are vital for the power of the political parties. They are sources of finance and employment for the dominant regime of Socialist Democrats, Socialists, Republicans, and Liberals;
- the public sector credit institutions, which control over 60 per cent of all deposits, provide money for politically inspired public works;
- privatisation would mean restructuring and job losses, which are not popular with the general public and so not with the political parties either.

In addition, legal and informal barriers have prevented private sector competition with public sector companies. The search for capital has forced public holding companies to seek private funds through the sale of minority holdings. Although IRI has raised billions through stock market offerings, little more than 20 per cent of this has derived from full privatisations.

The Financial Times reported in October 1990 that Franco Piga, minister for state shareholdings, sees a number of additional obstacles to privatisation including:

- the backwardness of the Italian stock market;

- lack of financial products;

- insider trading and other manipulations;

- lack of proper protection for minority shareholders.

According to Piga, public companies which floated minority rights on the stock exchange are returning price/earnings ratios which remain below the market average. This suggests that the market puts a lower value on companies with state shareholdings.

The Netherlands

A coherent summary of the gameplan of the Dutch Government was given by Adrian Van den Ven, secretary of the Interministerial Committee on Privatisation, in July 1988:

The vigorous approach to privatisation which is enshrined in the policy accord of the present coalition government shows that the Netherlands is in step with international developments as outlined above. After a brief study period, a start was made on privatisation in 1982 when the first Lubbers government [a coalition of Christian Democrats and

Liberals] took office. Privatisation is one element in a policy of reorganising the public sector. When the first Lubbers government took office, public expenditure was absorbing 71 per cent of national income, and the budget deficit exceeded 10 per cent. Public expenditure has now been reduced to approximately 63 per cent of national income, and a target of approximately 5.25 per cent has been set for the budget deficit of 1990.

Under the first Lubbers government, a number of privatisation projects were started, and in some cases also completed. Under the second Lubbers government, which took office in 1986, privatisation policy has been pursued 'vigorously', as the coalition policy accord put it. Many projects were completed by the end of the government's term of office in 1990. Some 120 000 public servants have moved to the private sector. The target set for revenue from sales of state holdings in private enterprise was in the region of DFl2 billion, and this figure is likely to be exceeded by more than DFl1 billion.

In practice, the Netherlands has a relatively low state ownership of industry. The reason, says Van den Ven, is that 'Unlike the United Kingdom and France, the Netherlands has never had periods when nationalisation was fashionable.'

Under the first Lubbers government, the possibilities of disposing of state holdings in about forty companies were reviewed and a start was made on a programme of gradual sales in cases where this course was regarded as acceptable on grounds of policy and from the financial point of view. Until 1986, relatively limited packages of shares in KLM, Nederlandse Middenstandsbank, Hoogovens, and a number of other smaller holdings were sold off (for a total price in the region of DFl500 million).

Under the second Lubbers government, policy on selling off assets has been developed further. The coalition policy accord anticipated that revenue from sales of state holdings over the whole of the government's term of office would exceed DFl2 billion. Most of this would be derived from the sale of one-third of the shares in DSM, which was wholly owned by the state. The sale went ahead at the beginning of 1989 and yielded approximately DFl1.3 billion. The sale of another third of the original holding took place in November 1989.

The status of those companies with government equity holdings in mid-1988 is summarised in the table below:

Table 2.2   Dutch government equity holdings, mid-1988

Name	Value DFl 1000 govt. share	Share in total capital (%)	Status
Postbank	300 000	100	merger with NMB bank proposed, government share 49% or less
Bank voor Nederl. Gemeenten (Bank Netherlands Local Councils)	164 796	50	unchanged
Nationale Invest-erings Bank (National Investment Bank)	50 333	50.3	share will be held at 50.3%
KLM	487 915	39	share will be held at 39%, option majority share available
Hoogovens (Steel industry)	53 905	14	share will be sold

Table 2.2   Continued

Name	Value DFI 1000 govt. share	Share in total capital (%)	Status
Vredestein (tyre industry)	21 266	49	share will be sold
Schiphol Airport	129 880	76	unchanged
Ultra Centrifuge Nederland (nuclear energy)	161 400	99	under discussion
DSM (Chemical sector)	700 000	100	one third of share will be sold
Nederlandse Energie ontwikkelingsmij (energy development)	55 900	100	unchanged
Nederlandse daughter company Van Gend en Loos has been sold	484 438	100	Govt asked management NS for further plans
Maatschappij voor Industriele Projecten (Capital Venture Fund)	330 000	57	unchanged

The main thrust of privatisation, however, has been in the big, wholly-owned state enterprises. The Postbank was spun out of the PTT as a separate limited company, with the government diluting its equity stake to a minority shareholding. The PTT has also been formed into an autonomous company, but a decision still has to be reached as to whether it is to be privatised. The Government Printing and Publishing Office has followed the same path and is due to be privatised within five years of gaining plc status. The Mint is also being examined as a candidate for privatisation. The only one of these enterprises to have been sold off by 1989 was The Ijmuiden Fishing Port Authority, which was sold to a private sector company in which provincial and municipal authorities have a minority holding. If all of these enterprises are privatised, more than 100 000 employees will pass from the public to the private sector.

In terms of numbers of privatisations, though not value, the most common area for disposals has been government agencies. These agencies represent another 21 000 civil servants transferred to the private sector or otherwise taken out of direct government control.

Like the United Kingdom, the Netherlands has a strong programme encouraging contracting out by both civil service departments and local authorities. Unlike the UK, however, it has made very little use of flotation as a means of privatising wholly-owned enterprises, the only example to date being the public offer for the first tranche of one-third of the shares of DSM (formerly Dutch State Mines). This issue, which gave priority to small shareholders and to DSM employees, attracted strong interests from overseas, as well as domestically.

The DSM sale followed the pattern which has become common in Britain. A great deal of advertising, including roadshows around the country, aroused interest to the extent that the offer was oversubscribed by six times. By contrast, the previous flotation of part of the state's holding in airline KLM had seen most of the shares bought by overseas investors. (Although the Government reduced its stake in KLM to 39 per cent from 55 per cent, it reserved the right to regain control whenever it wishes.)

Portugal

The impetus for privatisation in Portugal was the accession of a Social Democrat government in 1987, with a mandate to return large sectors of industry to the private sector. The nationalised sector was extensive, owing to a nationalisation programme following the 1974 revolution, which left virtually every branch of economic activity under state rule.

First the Portuguese had to change the constitution, which did not allow denationalisation. Before 1987, the Portuguese constitution declared that the nationalisations carried out in 1975 were irreversible — 49 per cent of the equity had to stay in public hands. This limitation had kept away most potential buyers. An agreement between Portugal's ruling Social Democrat party and the Socialists enabled the government to go ahead with plans to sell off some of the substantial interests it controls in Portuguese industry. The agreement stated that proceeds of any sale of state assets can only be used for productive investments or the reduction of the public debt, not for ordinary budget expenses. It also guaranteed priority purchasing rights to employees of the firms that were to be sold.

Between 1976 and 1987 the nationalised firms had been dependent on large cash injections, but by the late 'eighties most of the firms were showing signs of recovery and were looking ripe for sale. For example, in 1982, state-owned firms needed the equivalent of 11.4 per cent of the nation's GNP to keep going. By 1987, this aid was down to 2 per cent.

The government did not announce the overall programme at once, but privatised gradually. The nationalised companies were valued by two firms, who made separate appraisals. International auditors analysed their balance sheets in detail.

The results of the valuations and proposals by the companies' boards of directors were then submitted to the government. The Council of Ministers determined the value of these companies and established the conditions for the privatisation.

One of the most recent privatisations was of the brewing company, Unicer, which had been part-privatised some time before. The government had retained a 51 per cent majority and, in offering this to the public, imposed limits on the proportion of equity that could be subscribed by overseas investors. In the event, although the offer was technically oversubscribed by 65 per cent, in reality the underwriters were left with nearly 5 per cent of the shares because of a shortfall in demand from domestic small investors.

Among the state-owned companies up for sale is the national airline, TAP. Nationalised in 1975, TAP had made losses every year since and was technically bankrupt, with its liabilities exceeding its assets. A relatively small airline, with only twenty-nine aircraft, TAP was nonetheless an attractive bait for American and European airlines, because of its strong links with South America (particularly Brazil) and Africa.

The main cause of TAP's problems appears to have been constant interference in its management by successive governments. The company suffered a series of rapid changes in top management, and was prevented from undertaking essential rationalisations, such as discontinuing unprofitable routes, because of the impact this would have had on employment. In the past four years, however, more stable management and a relaxation of political control have enabled the company to start to reduce manpower levels, which are, however, still too high for the size of the business. Combined with membership of the European Community and the stronger escudo, these management changes have helped the company return to operating profit; but the level of debt hinders expansion and modernization of an ageing fleet. A new injection of capital from flotation or a strategic alliance with a major overseas airline appeared suitable options for recovery. Part of the preparation for privatisation will be a gradual opening up of the internal airline market to greater competition, and the phasing out of government subsidies on loss-making routes to Madeira and the Azores — both moves that will force further rationalisation.

By the end of 1990, the Portuguese government faced some important questions over the future of its ambitious privatisation programme when it failed to find sufficient buyers for the state brewer, Centralcer. The healthy organisation has 50 per cent of the Portuguese beer market, a share of the wine market and a growing business in soft drinks. It produces well-known drinks such as Carlsberg under licence, and its Agua de Luso brand has a 41 per cent share of the local mineral-water market. The company's sales were Es19.8 billion ($147 million) in 1988, but since 1988, profits have risen by almost 200 per cent. In theory, Centralcer should have been attractive to a broad range of investors, but it left its underwriters with over 35 per cent of the issue. An additional complication in this case was the company's former owners. They were fighting in the courts to stop the sale, claiming they should be given back at least 43 per cent of their company or much better compensation. Key reasons for the failure include:

- The decline of the Portuguese equity market from a peak in January 1990. This was a consequence of the Gulf crisis and world economic slowdown;

- An emphasis on stock market flotation instead of direct negotiations with prospective buyers;

- Greed. The inflated share price was intended to enable the government to raise maximum revenue from privatisation;

- Foreign institutions are only allowed to buy a limited amount of shares. In the past, foreign investors got round this by making alliances with local partners. But the policy is viewed as arbitrary, counter-productive and bureaucratic.

Many of Portugal's heavyweight privatisations have been left until last. In December 1990, the government floated the last 33 per cent of Banco Portugues de Atlantico, the largest state-owned commercial bank. The government is also planning the first phase of the privatisation of the oil group, Petrogal, through a capital increase. During 1991 we shall see the privatisation of six banks, including Banco Espirito Santo e Commercial de Lisboa, the second largest state-owned commercial bank, and three insurance companies, including the country's largest, Mundial Confianaca and Imperio. Other significant issues will include Cimentos di Portugal and Secil, two cement groups, Siderugia Nacional, the steel group and CTT/TLP, the telephone company.

Portuguese capital alone will not be able to absorb such large-scale stock floating. The government may well be forced to allow foreign groups a greater role in the process. It may also have to make concessions to former owners.

Sweden

Sweden has a relatively small state sector, which is being restructured under a government policy of partial privatisation. Sweden's state sector employs no more than about 100 000 workers, and its contribution to the gross national product remains low. The government plans to create a holding company, which will be 85 per cent state owned. The rest will be sold off to public pension funds and wage-earner funds in the form of convertible loans. Under the scheme, the state plans to reduce its controlling interest in any of the holdings where it still holds a majority of shares without needing the prior consent of parliament.

Procordia is a key example of this partial privatision policy. The company introduced a new core business strategy in 1984. It pulled out of loss-making activities in mining, steel, forestry and textiles, and concentrated on building up its strength in consumer products like pharmaceuticals, tobacco, beer, food and hotels. It was partially floated on the stock market in the autumn of 1987 and is now discussing sharing ownership with Volvo. In schemes such as this, the Swedish policy aims to mix the public and private in a bid to meet the increasing internationalisation of business.

Table 2.3 Sweden's state industrial sector

Sector	Equity votes	State share (SKr m)	Profits	Turn-over	Staff
NCB (Forestry)	51	62	271	4.02	3 751
SSAB (Steel)	40	50.2	1 146	13.25	12 801
Assi (Packaging)	100	100	466	6.22	7 186
LKAB (Mining)	100	100	291	6.24	3 921
FFV (Defence)	100	100	291	4.68	10 037
Celsius (Combine)	100	100	10	8.68	10 384
Procordia (Combine)	33	41	1 991	18.22	27 834

(*Source: Robert Taylor,* The Financial Times, November 1990)

Spain

Spain began privatising in earnest in 1985. Our case studies of SEAT (page 93) and Repsol (page 167) explore Spanish privatisation in more depth.

Turkey

In Turkey, privatisation is a major plank of government strategy, although activity has slowed. The plan got off to a flying start in 1984 with the partial privatisation of the Bosporus Bridge, which links Asia and Europe, and the Keban Hydroelectric Dam. These first sell-offs were keenly received by the general public and shares were oversubscribed.

However, according to the American research institute, the Centre for Privatisation, the government faces resistance from bureaucrats, unions and local politicians. Privatisation is also unattractive because of numerous economic restrictions such as import barriers, price controls and a restrictive interest policy. The collapse of the Istanbul stock exchange in 1987–88 and the disastrous sale of Teletas put investors off buying into state-run companies. Undaunted, in 1988 the government decided to gradually privatise SumerBank, a textiles conglomerate, and Petkim, a petrochemicals giant.

West Germany

When Helmut Kohl became Chancellor in 1982 he announced an extensive programme of privatisation. The state held shareholdings of 25 per cent or more in 958 companies and these shareholdings were gradually whittled down over the following five years.

There was a temporary blip while the programme overcame the effects of the stock market crash in 1987 and the foreign exchange scandal at Volkswagen, which held up the sale of the remaining 16 per cent of that company's equity. However, the pace of selling continued into the 1990s, with major sales including 26 per cent of equity in Veba, the oil and chemicals conglomerate, for $1.4 billion. (For details about privatisation in the former East Germany, see Chapter 5, Eastern Europe, page 75.)

Israel

In 1985, when Israel tried to tackle its raging inflation and giant deficits, the intention was to dismantle the state's role in the economy in favour of a more market-oriented system. The 170 government-owned companies made up some 12 per cent of economic activity, but their profit level was poor, with overall return on capital in 1988 of less than two per cent. Both Likud and Labour, the two main parties, were in favour of denationalisation. American investment companies wrote a blueprint for the sale of twenty-five state companies. The aim was to sell through private placement, public offering, or a mixture of the two. Included in the disposal plans were the state telecommunications monopoly, electricity, and Israel Chemicals, the most profitable state enterprise. El Al, the airline, and Israel Aircraft Industries were also in line to be sold.

Objections have arisen, not about the idea of privatisation, but about the way it should be carried out. Objectors dislike the concept of private placement of government holdings, but the Tel Aviv stock exchange is so small a private placement is necessary. The Finance Ministry has already managed to push through the sale of a 75 per cent stake in Paz Oil to an Australian investor for $100 million. It later sold over 80 per cent of the Jerusalem Economic Corporation, a property company, for more than $54 million. Objectors claimed the price was too low and that the negotiations were made in secret.

When the government tried to sell a 50 per cent stake in Israel Chemicals (worth over $400 million) to a foreign buyer, the Knesset Finance Committee blocked the move. Israel Chemicals exports Israel's only natural resource, potash, and the committee was opposed to the foreign ownership of a strategic resource. Instead, the Finance Committee favoured a public offering followed by the private sale of a small stake.

Several small flotations have already been completed. Maman, an air cargo handling company, sold 49 per cent. Plans are also afoot to partially privatise El Al and the state telecommunications agency. The state also has majority shareholdings in most of the country's main banks. It is planning to sell off its stake in the Bank of Leumi, Israel Discount Bank, Bank Mizrahi and Bank Hapoalim. Trade-offs with present owners and managers are likely to limit the opportunities for outsiders in the sale.

3

NORTH AND SOUTH AMERICA

Argentina

Argentina's recent forays into privatisation have been stimulated in large part by the desperate need to stem the flow of
public capital into loss-making giants. The nationalised industries showed a loss of nearly $4 billion in 1989 — about the
equivalent of the country's trade surplus for the entire year.
According to *The Financial Times* (17 May 1990), fully a third
of the deficit was accounted for by one enterprise, the telephone company, ENTel.

For that reason alone, ENTel was one of the first enterprises
to be put up for sale. The original intention was to sell 60 per
cent of the enterprise by January 1990 to foreign investors,
who would agree to inject $4 billion in further investment
over the next ten years. A major part of the deal was that the
banks which supported the seven overseas telecoms companies bidding for the ENTel stake would write off $3.5 billion of
Argentinean debt against the equity acquired. For the banks
the sale was a good opportunity to write off losses, for
Argentina's debt is valued at only 12 cents in the dollar on
secondary currency markets. However, the January deadline
came and went, being replaced with a new deadline of June,
then October 1990.

In early 1991 ENTel's sale went ahead relatively smoothly,
if late. But the privatisation programme, regarded by President

Menem as a central plank of his economic recovery strategy, is receiving a rough ride elsewhere. Although polls indicate that 70 per cent of Argentineans support the programme, which will take out of public ownership the thirteen largest state enterprises, there is loud criticism of the manner in which it has been pursued. When two television channels were privatised at the end of 1989 there were accusations of corruption. Plans to privatise trunk roads under a scheme that would have leased them to contractors, who could charge tolls to cover the costs of maintenance, came in for similar treatment and have been put on the back burner, along with plans to privatise parts of the railway system.

Foreign banks are looking to the privatisation programme for more debt-equity conversion deals like the ENTel one. These banks hold almost $40 billion of the country's foreign debt. Argentina has paid no commercial bank interest on medium-term loans since April 1988. In April 1990, the Argentinean Private Development Trust (APDT) was created with a $1.2 billion fund to handle Argentine debt-equity swaps resulting from the privatisation and deregulation programme.

The APDT was formed by Midland Bank, Banco Rio de la Plata Argentina, the Bank of Tokyo and the International Finance Corporation (IFC), the world bank affiliate promoting private ventures in developing countries. It represents for shareholders the first creative opening towards getting something in return for their withered Argentine loans. The Argentine government also stands to gain because:

- it can hand over turbulent management problems at state-run companies;

- it gets rid of nationalised industry deficits;

- it shifts on to the banks the future investment requirements of the debt-swamped nationalised companies.

However, even with a debt-equity swap mechanism in place, attempts to privatise the national airline, Aerolineas Argentinas, have hit other hurdles. Eighty-five per cent of the troubled airline was put up for sale as a package for $220 million, and a debt-equity exchange of at least $1500 million. First SAS pursued a deal, finally giving up in exasperation after two years of fruitless negotiation. Then American Airlines and Iberia expressed interest in purchasing the airline, the latter in partnership with a local conglomerate, whose chief executive, according to *The Financial Times*, was 'engaged in a personal feud with' the Minister of Public Works, who had responsibility for the sale. American Airlines pulled out in June 1990 to compete head-on with the Argentinean carrier. The empty space at the negotiating table was taken by a consortium consisting of the Dutch airline KLM, the Brazilian airline Varig, and Chase Manhattan.

The sale eventually went ahead in November 1990. Iberia headed a consortium which picked up 85 per cent of the shares. Negotiations continued right up until the last minute. In the final purchase Iberia took a 30 per cent stake in the consortium and introduced new unnamed foreign investors to take a 19 per cent stake, giving itself a 49 per cent share in the consortium in all. Aerolineas staff hold 10 per cent and the government holds a 5 per cent stake. The consortium paid $130 million cash and a further $130 million over five years, plus over $2 billion in foreign debt certificates which it must deliver in ninety days. In addition, Iberia promised to find international banks to guarantee the investment programme and the $130 million deferred payments. The government also required the buyers to invest $683 million in the airline over five years.

Brazil

A privatisation plan was announced by the Sarney administration upon taking office in 1985. By 1989, 26 out of 415 companies were expected to be sold.

The plan has run into difficulties for a number of reasons. Firstly, recent labour problems, especially in the steel industry; and secondly, an overshadowing inflation crisis. The image of privatisation in Brazil was further damaged with the cancellation of the auction of Mafersa, a wholly state-owned bus and rolling stock manufacturer. President Sarney stopped the auction scheduled for October 1989 after allegations that the company had been intentionally undervalued. Allegations over Mafersa centre on a decision to fix a floor price on the company of $20 million, despite calculations that it was worth $39 million. The sale of Camacari Chemicals and the Cariba copper mine were both postponed indefinitely following this scandal.

Canada

Canada has a modest privatisation programme, which has not been helped by poor trading conditions on the world's markets. For example, the privatisation of Cameco, the Canadian Mining and Energy Company, an Ontario based group that is the world's largest supplier of uranium, had to be postponed in 1990 because of the depressed market for its product.

Chile

'The breadth of the privatisations in Chile would leave even some of Mrs Thatcher's divestment zealots feeling like failures. In fact, one independent study covering the period until

September 1988 concluded that, taking into account the relative size of both economies, Chile had transferred twice the value of state assets to the private sector than Britain, and in half the time.' So said *The Financial Times* (11 April 1990).

Privatisation in Chile arose in the mid-1970s partly as a reaction against the nationalisation programme of the Socialist government of President Allende, partly as a means of generating income. Allende's government had appropriated or otherwise acquired large chunks of the private sector, to make it 60 per cent of the total economy.

When General Pinochet came to power in 1973 he privatised 350 companies within the first year, raising approximately $1 billion. The first batch of privatisations was followed by two more. The state holding company CORFU privatised 16 banks and 135 other companies in the following decade, raising a further $1 billion. The final batch of privatisations took place between 1985 and the restoration of democracy in 1989. During this period Chile began to move into the private sector. The Pinochet doctrine differed from that of most of Latin America, in that it permitted — even encouraged — foreign participation in the privatised companies.

The public sector has now shrunk to 40 per cent of the gross domestic product. Relatively little now remains to be sold — the largest exporting enterprise, copper mining, remains in public hands and was not seriously considered as a privatisation candidate because it contributed too much to foreign currency earnings. Moreover, the present government, while not openly hostile to all privatisation, is not enthusiastic.

Mexico

Mexico has one of the most extensive privatisation programmes in Latin America. It adopted the slow route and kept the big privatisations until the end.

Between 1983 and 1988, President Miquel de la Madrid disincorporated (that is, privatised or liquidated) about 600 state companies. Of these only 150 were sold, and most of these were small or bankrupt. By June 1988 the privatised companies had only raised $500 million. His successor, President Salinas, came to power in December 1988. By November 1990, his government had completed over 60 privatisations, mostly of larger companies. Perhaps to forestall criticism, workers have been given cheap shares.

The Salinas government has privatised the airline Mexicana and sold off a number of mining companies, including Cananea for $475 million. It has privatised a transport company for $80 million, some sugar mills also for $80 million, and a couple of steel and iron companies for about $70 million. Since June 1988 another $2.5 billion has been raised from sales.

The government also sold its stake in Telmex, the state telephone company, in December 1990. Telmex was a profitable company and a desirable purchase. It had enormous potential because of the underdevelopment of Mexico's telecommunications. Telmex stock recorded a 77 per cent rise. This reflected profits of 2660 billion pesos ($773 million) during the year, an increase of 75 per cent in real terms over the same period in 1989.

The government had previously burdened Telmex with a levy averaging 35 per cent on sales rather than profits, with varying rates for different services. In general, Mexican telecommunications had suffered from a lack of investment and had become one of the most backward aspects of the Mexican economy.

However, in advance of the sale, Telmex had stepped up investment, putting over 2000 billion pesos into construction in the first eight months of 1990. This compared favourably with under 1500 billion pesos invested in the same period in 1989. The company had taken its first step away from monopoly when it went into competition with eight countrywide cellular telephone concessionaires in February 1990. In 1996, the market will open to long distance carriers.

The finance minister also plans to raise $10 billion from privatisations in 1991 through the sale of the banks, the state steel company Sidermex, and the state fertiliser company. Most people thought that the banks would not be put on sale until after August 1991 and the crucial federal elections, but they were sold earlier than that because the $4–6 billion from their sale helped pay off up to a tenth of Mexico's internal debt. The government hoped to reduce inflation at the same time by reducing the size of this debt. Since the government was majority owner of the banks then it was seen, rightly or wrongly, as implicit guarantor of them all. The Mexicans are also taken with the idea of one-stop banking. Commercial banks cannot form groups with insurance companies and brokerages until the government sold its stake. Unlike previous privatisations, foreign investors were allowed up to 30 per cent of the banks' equity. The announcement of banking privatisation had an added bonus, in that it increased business confidence and brought interest rates down.

In preparation for the sell-off, the government liberalised the banking sector. Banks can now set deposit and lending rates, cut reserve requirements, and eliminate compulsory credit channelling to preferred sectors, but they could not truly compete until the government sold its majority shareholding.

In the year to July 1990, the eighteen nationalised banks collectively made $1 billion. The biggest bank, Banamex, made $175 million, Bancomer $131 million, and Serfin $123 million. But, according to Damian Fraser in *The Financial Times* in November 1990, banks may cease to be such profit centres. Firstly, although over the past five years there had been huge margins between borrowing and lending — as high as 10 per cent and averaging half of that — within two years the spread is predicted to fall to just 1.5 per cent.

Secondly, the government budget deficit has been huge, averaging 12 per cent of gross domestic product from 1982 to

1988. By 1988, the government had taken 50 per cent of all bank loans. In 1982, money market funds comprised 7 per cent of the broad money supply; by 1988 they made up 40 per cent of this total. This has been no-risk debt for the banks. But thanks to privatisation receipts, the government may run a deficit in 1991 of just 1–2 per cent of GDP.

Thirdly, inflation has been high and banks have managed to pocket some of the 'inflation tax' which arises when current accounts pay no interest. But if the austerity programme works, inflation will fall and that source of income will vanish.

In addition, all banks will have to relearn credit risk analysis as the private sector takes over from the public sector as the biggest borrower. Successful organisations will start to develop and securitise Mexico's almost non-existent mortgage market. Many may expand into mergers and acquisitions, venture capital and credit cards, all of which are immature and profitable markets in Mexico.

In the past, the Mexicans had sold off their state assets by closed auction. During 1988 and 1989, the government rejected the highest bidder at least three times at the final stage of the auction; on other occasions, the highest bidder dropped out and the whole process had to be started again. For the large privatisations, such as the sale of the banks and Telmex, potential buyers have to pass a pre-qualifying round and pay a deposit to enter it. Success in this round is determined by how solvent the buyers are, how much market power they may have, and their expertise. The pre-qualifiers then attend the auction. This two-stage programme gives investor and the government time to evaluate the companies and make suitable commitments.

Among other companies put up for sale are Aseguradora Mexicana, the country's largest insurance group, and silver-mining Compania Real del Monte y Pachuca. Compania Real is one of the oldest silver mines in the world, having been worked since Aztec times and continuously for nearly five hundred years. In recent years it has made heavy losses and seen its workforce halved. Put up for sale in August 1989, it was due to be transferred to a consortium of private sector companies early in 1990. The new owners paid $75 million.

Aseguradora is one of Mexico's top twenty-five companies and, unlike Compania Real, is a strong, profitable enterprise. It is likely to raise in excess of $150 million for the government, and is one of the first privatisations under which, as a result of recent regulatory changes, foreign companies can acquire holdings of up to 49 per cent.

In spite of all this activity the Mexican privatisation programme is not quite the wholesale sell-off it may first appear. Oil, electricity and postal services are to remain in the public sector.

USA

Privatisation in the USA is not the issue that it is in other countries. The political system has always leant towards the free market rather than central economic control, so a large state-owned sector has never developed. Nonetheless, there have been major privatisations, such as that of Amtrac, the rail network. In addition, many local authorities already contract out services such as cemeteries, prisons and crime patrols. Contracting out became even more widespread when the government cut federal subsidies in the 1960s.

4

ASIA AND THE PACIFIC

Australia and New Zealand

The Australian Government recently announced plans to part-privatise the Commonwealth Bank of Australia, selling an estimated 30 per cent of the shares. The money will be used to acquire another financial institution, the State Bank of Victoria, whose viability was heavily undermined by the collapse of its merchant banking subsidiary, Tricontinental, with losses reported to be A$500 million. The government is also selling 40 per cent of its stake in Qantas, its international airline, and Australina Airlines, the state-owned domestic carrier. The state's debt-laden Aussat satellite company is also to be sold. As is commonly the case, the sale of the airlines will have restrictions on foreign ownership. To offset the negative effects of state ownership, the government was also looking at ways to expose Telecom Australia, the domestic telephone utility, to competition.

In New Zealand too, privatisation is increasingly seen as a solution to excessive state ownership. There, the Labour government has agreed to sell a minority share in Telecom Corporation, restructure the railways for sale, and study selling off the international airports. The government plans to retain a controlling share in Telecom Corporation, while selling a substantial proportion overseas.

Bangladesh

Here the government divested over a thousand companies between 1976 and 1984. In 1982 alone, thirty-three jute and twenty-seven textile mills were returned to their former owners. Entrepreneurs have bought some of the manufacturing and chemical companies. Other enterprises, including some banks, were sold through public offerings.

The privatisation programme took place in four phases:

- gradual disinvestment of public enterprises;

- disinvestment of some state units (total sell-out);

- transfer of remaining jute and textile mills to their original owners;

- public sale of 49 per cent of the shares of the public sector enterprises.

In the case of disinvestment, assets are sold against the highest bids on tenders, and liabilities remain in the hands of the government. Shares are floated at current market value. If the government retains 51 per cent of the shares, 15 per cent are earmarked for employees and 34 per cent are sold to the public. The government has also awarded management contracts — for example, it signed over the Bangladesh Machine Tools Factory Ltd to the Belgian firm Fabrique Nationale Herstal SA.

India

The Indian administration announced limited privatisation measures as part of a plan to meet the country's fiscal and balance-of-payments crises in late 1990. In this way, the government hopes to avoid large-scale borrowing from the

International Monetary Fund. According to senior ministers, the proposals will allow public sector groups like Air India and the Oil and Natural Gas Commission to bring in private shareholders by raising funds through the stock market which would dilute the equity. (*The Financial Times*, David Housego, 24 December 1990.)

Thailand

Thailand has had a policy of restricting the number of state enterprises since the 1960s, when the government decided to foster the growth of the private sector. This has led to a decline in state-owned companies from one hundred in 1960 to sixty-seven in 1987. The government aims to privatise a proportion of the remaining enterprises, but it has run into difficulties. Enterprises like the Electricity Authority of Thailand and the Telephone Organisation of Thailand are saddled with 60 per cent of the country's foreign debt, and the private sector doesn't want them.

Indonesia

Indonesia has 215 privatised companies with combined assets of more than $68 billion that account for more than 80 per cent of the country's economic activity. These companies occupy every industrial niche, including oil and gas, utilities, plantations, mining, manufacturing, textiles, construction and banking. The majority of these operate at a loss. According to the Centre for Privatisation's *Privatisation Survey for Developing Countries*, a sharp decrease in oil prices and rapid increase in the operating costs of public firms has caused the government to consider privatisation as a valid strategy to decrease deficits.

In June 1989, the government revealed possible plans for the state companies which included privatisation, joint ventures with the private sector, and liquidation. In November that year, it announced that fifty-two nationalised ventures would be sold. However, there has been stiff resistance to the plan.

Malaysia

The Centre for Privatisation reports that Malaysia's programme, intended to be one of the most extensive of its kind in the developing world, has not progressed very far since its creation in 1985. The government owns about nine hundred companies, spread across all sectors of the economy. It has offered more than seventy loss-makers at a discount, and more are planned.

In June 1988, the government called in an international consortium of bankers, lawyers and accountants to lay down a privatisation policy framework and an action plan for the privatisation of over two hundred organisations within the next ten years. By 1990, only thirteen projects had been completed, including the much-publicised flotation of the Malaysian International Shipping Corporation and the partial privatisation of the Malaysian Airline System. (Source: Centre for Privatisation, *Privatisation Survey for Developing Countries*, March 1990)

Pakistan

Benazir Bhutto's government commissioned a report on the viability of an extensive privatisation programme when she took over in late 1988. Following the report, the government's National Divestment Authority launched a privatisation campaign prior to a share sell-off in 1991. Pakistan's state-owned companies are over-manned and a great drain on the nation's resources. President Zia had earlier undertaken a similar divestment programme which ran into difficulties when he offloaded both the company and its debts. In addition, the current capital market does not have the capacity to support any large-scale projects. A volatile political atmosphere in the country has also hampered the private sector.

Following the fall of Bhutto, the new government under Prime Minister Nawaz Sharif is continuing the process of denationalisation. In early 1991, it passed laws on denationalisation of the banks, and has already started to privatise the Muslim Commercial Bank. It also announced that it will sell off 115 public sector organisations within a year.

Philippines

Following the Marcos era, privatisation was seen as a reform that reduced corruption and increased accountability. In late 1986, President Aquino introduced a programme to value, package and market many of the government-held assets.

To interest investors, debt-equity swap programmes with attractive terms were introduced by the Central Bank of the Philippines. Foreign investors can buy a portion of the Philippines external debt and receive pesos at a premium for investment in selected areas. This programme has proved a major success. The government sought a $200 million World Bank loan to finance privatisation of its corporations. The rationalisation programme plans to cut the number of state-run concerns from 296 to 40. Among them is Philippines Airlines.

Progress has been slow, however. A number of the assets for sale are non-operating, loss making, under litigation or facing legal impediments, such as injunctions or sequestration. The requirements of the Commission on Audits before and after a sale are also cumbersome. Lastly, some of the nationalised companies are headed by officials who refuse to yield their positions and are devising ways to forestall the process.

Singapore and South Korea

Singapore now has a divestment committee, which recommended a massive ten-year privatisation programme. In South Korea, the government has privatised all commercial banks and sold large industrial organisations to the private sector.

5

EASTERN EUROPE

Czechoslovakia

The Czech Government is looking to devise a scheme to privatise its economy, the most thoroughly nationalised of all the former Communist states, but it is not easy. Dusan Triska, senior advisor at the finance ministry, explained his problem to *The Financial Times* in June 1990: 'If we tried to use a standard method of privatisation, it would take hundreds of years. To get the companies in good shape before coming to the market, like the British did, would mean a consulting agency for each one. It would take two or three years each and would cost millions.'

The government has decided to try auctioning. January 1991 saw the auction of the first twenty premises in Prague city hall. Plans are afoot to sell more than a hundred thousand retail businesses in this fashion. The Czechs hope to foster competition by breaking the link between retail shops and the central warehouses or producers supplying them. Properties claimed by the original owner will not be placed on auction, and foreigners are barred from bidding in the first rounds as the goal is to place property in private Czechoslovak hands.

Eastern Germany

Industry in Eastern Germany — some eight thousand companies — is up for sale in its entirety. In 1990, the government
appointed a leading Western German industrialist, Detlev
Rohwedder, chairman of steel company Hoesch, to master-
mind the sell-off. Rohwedder, who was assassinated in early
1991, was appointed chairman of the Treuhandanstalt, a trust
that owns most of the firms in Eastern Germany. Another
Western German industrialist, Reiner Gohlke, former head of
Western Germany's railways, was appointed as chief executive of Treuhand, only to resign in August as the complexities
and political exposure of the job took their toll. Set up in
March 1990, by the end of the year it had sold only about forty
companies and found prospective buyers for about two
hundred.

Deutsche Bank and Allianz between them carved up Eastern
Germany's banking and insurance sectors. The Treuhand has
blocked Western German takeover of parts of the Eastern
German retail network, and the proposal of Lufthansa to take a
controlling stake in Interflug, the Eastern German airline (the
latter on the grounds of reduced competition). Negotiations for
the airline took so long that it went into liquidation in 1991.

The Treuhand is also lending money to restructure firms. It
plans to close at least two thousand companies which have no
long-term chance of survival, according to *The Financial
Times* (October 1990). European building materials firms are
busy negotiating to take over major Eastern German building
groups such as Rudersdorf and the cement manufacturer
Karlsdorf. Interest stems from the fact that the Eastern German
building market is predicted to grow rapidly over the next few
years as public and private investment in infrastructure
increases.

The process is complicated by hundreds of thousands of
individual claims on former state assets. The Treuhand has to
sell 1.8 million hectares of agricultural land, a mammoth task

which would take over forty-five years at the average rate of land disposal in Western Germany.

In some cases — for example, the electricity takeovers — there has been concern over the creation of monopolies, and the Western German cartel office has raised objections. However, the political will to unite as rapidly as possible seems to have been stronger. By 1991, Eastern German electricity production and transport were handed over to a body which is majority controlled by the three big German power companies, RWE, Preussenelektra and Bayernwerk. They will hold between 60 per cent and 75 per cent of the capital, with up to 25 per cent of this reserved for five medium-sized Western German power groups. About 15 per cent is held by a foreign consortium, which is led by Électricité de France and includes Tractabel of Belgium, Endesa of Spain and EOS of Switzerland.

Many former owners are reclaiming their family businesses. According to *The Independent* (John Eisenhammer, April 1990) owners are buying back their companies for the price the government paid for them. Adam Ice, one company which has been reprivatised, typifies many of the problems. The son is running the factory with the help of his father, who built the firm, but unfortunately neither has had any experience of management or marketing. Organisations such as the Association of Small and Medium Sized Firms have been set up to help owners overcome these initial problems.

However, many Eastern German companies will not be able to survive competition from the West and will go out of business. One reason is that currency union hit foreign sales of Eastern German goods. Priced in Deutschmarks they become uncompetitive overnight. At the same time, Eastern Germans shunned domestic products in favour of Western goods.

Floundering, newly-founded companies received over DM11 billion and were granted a flat rate of 41 per cent to all liquidity requests by the Treuhand. This propped up doomed businesses at the expense of potentially viable companies. To prevent such a drain on resources, Rohwedder ordered that companies look for financing from the banks rather than from the state, and that they must complete proper accounts and business orders. The organisation also has to take into account charges that Western Germany is gobbling up Eastern German assets and shutting out foreign investors.

Many companies are unable to put forward concrete proposals to buy because Eastern German companies have not submitted proper accounts. Statistics available on the companies for sale give only the barest of information and often do not even include the number of employees. To add to the confusion, the Eastern Germans have a penchant for splitting companies into several parts and giving each new organisation a separate name.

Investors can now seek help from independent consulting organisations such as Price Waterhouse, who now have members of their staff seconded to the Treuhand. The consultancy acts as an intermediary by finding buyers and advising several Eastern German concerns. Western bosses have also been drafted into the Treuhand to crack down on the regrouping of the *apparatchiks* of the old system and use their experience of free market economies.

According to *International Management* in February 1991, social responsibility is the Treuhand's heaviest burden. It has drawn up a list of doomed concerns, many of which are large employers. For example, five thousand jobs were lost with the closure of Pentacon, the Dresden-based producer of Practica cameras. Here the Treuhand worked with Pentacon representatives to retrain the workforce. It is hoped that the Pentacon experience will serve as a model for other situations.

Unemployment queues in Eastern Germany are predictably lengthening, however, since it is no longer possible to overstaff to achieve full employment. On the contrary, businesses must reduce their workforces if they wish to survive. Treuhand employees themselves are destined for the dole queue once their job is finished, though this will not be for some time since recent estimates predict that the sell-off will take at least ten to fifteen years to complete.

Hungary

Hungary's first privatisation, of part of the state travel agency Ibusz, ran into such severe controversy that it may have set back the entire programe. The agency was floated on the Austrian Stock Exchange and the Budapest Exchange. The share price trebled immediately trading began, leading Opposition critics to assert that it had been heavily underpriced and that the government was engaged in a 'selling-out of Hungarian national property', because Hungarians could not buy in Vienna. The furore had a swift and negative effect on the fledgling Budapest Stock Exchange. Ibusz shares fell sharply.

The Hungarian privatisation movement has been going longer than other Eastern Bloc countries. From 1988 onwards, it had been enacting modern company and foreign investment legislation, designed to lay the foundation for private enterprise and foreign investors. Much of the company law was modelled on the West German and Austrian models. Unlike some other countries, there is no limit to the amount of foreign ownership or management control, although approval is needed for majority foreign control. In 1989, it enacted specific privatisation legislation aimed at ensuring the orderly denationalisation of over two thousand enterprises.

The privatisation programme got under way in earnest in September 1990 when the State Property Agency announced the names of twenty state companies to be sold. The list included Hungarhotels, Danubius Hotel and Spa Company, and the rest of the Ibusz travel agency. The sales will either be through public share offering, employee share-ownership schemes, or competitive bidding.

Previous privatisations had been 'spontaneous', initiated by the state-owned enterprise's management under earlier reforms designed to build market socialism. Spontaneous privatisation will continue, but the hope is that controlled privatisation will set the general pattern and transfer 5—8 per cent of state property yearly.

Hungary's ailing engineering giants will also be for sale, among them companies such as bus manufacturers Ikarus and Csepel Auto, and Videoton, the electronics company. All are

Table 5.1   Hungarian companies due for privatisation

Company	Foreign inv.limit %	Equity ($m)	Assets ($m)	Turnover ($m)	Pre-tax profit ($m)
Richter Gedeon (Drugs)	33	139	291	260	16
Hungarhotels (Hotels)	50	55	182	125	16
MEH Trust (Recycling)	None	34	63	148	14
Pannonia (Hotels)	30	48	103	87	10
Danubius (Hotels)	50	41	111	65	9
Pannonplast (Plastics)	None	37	69	91	7
Centrum Stores (Retail)	30	45	87	310	7

in trouble and will need new technology and an overhauled management.

Poland

In the summer of 1990, Poland requested assistance from a number of countries in planning and implementing its privatisation programme. First off the mark, through the £50 billion Polish Know-How Fund, were several British organisations with experience in handling major privatisations. Among them were three merchant banks, Barclays de Zoete Wedd, N M Rothschild and Schroder Wragg, and accountants Ernst & Young and KPMG. The first task of these organisations was to identify the prime candidates for privatisation. A detailed account of Polish privatisation progress will be found on pages 235 to 241.

In mid-1990, the Polish parliament passed by an overwhelming majority a new law to facilitate privatisation. Under the law, a newly established Ministry of Property Transformation will select state organizations for privatisation. It will transform these organisations into joint stock companies and will move them into the private sector within two years of doing so.

The mechanisms for privatisation are still being evolved. The exercise revealed the extraordinary primitiveness of the financial sector. It has proved extremely difficult to privatise state-owned companies in the absence of a functioning banking system, stock exchange, brokers, prospectus or security printers, and an efficient telephone system. Extreme vagueness over the real ownership and legal status of assets does not help, either. The experts have tried to create clear laws and functioning financial and marketing institutions, and have tried to set a precedent by privatising the first companies in a rigorously documented way.

Foreign companies will be able to acquire 10 per cent of shares without special permission. The most radical proposal, however, is to issue vouchers to the entire adult population, allowing them to buy shares. This would make Poland the country with the world's largest per capita participation in share ownership. The law also allows for employees of an enterprise to buy up to 20 per cent of the shares at half price through an ESOP (employee share-ownership) scheme.

The first batch of companies to be privatised include the Prochnik textile works in Lodz, Exbud, an exporter of construction services, the Silesian Cable Works and Inowroclaw meat works. These were transformed into joint stock companies in late 1990.

Exbud has always been rather special in the Polish context. It was set up by Witold Zareska in 1978 with a borrowed one million zloty as the export sector of the local state building enterprise. Now Exbud employs over 11 000 people and earns export income of over £51 million. Exbud has always been run like a private company with Zareska at the helm. The plan is to sell a proportion of shares abroad, a proportion to the employees, some on the open market and the rest to Zareska and his top managers. The scheme in effect amounts to a management buy-out.

The Soviet Union

Although the Soviet Union has not yet sold off any significant enterprises, it has laid much of the groundwork for privatisation. Recent legislation by the Soviet government allows both domestic and foreign investors to buy stocks and bonds in Soviet enterprises. It is also planning to privatise over 1000 retail stores, 9300 public catering facilities, and 12 800 businesses in the service sector.

Commodity exchanges are functioning in many cities, three of them in Moscow, where a Stock Exchange has been started and where a foreign currency market is expected to be operating soon.

Yugoslavia

The Federal Agency for Privatisation is charged with the task of restructuring the existing enterprise sector ready for its sale. The privatisation law was passed in 1989 and refined in 1990. It allows Yugoslavs and foreigners far-reaching property rights. Before 1989, the workers had owned the enterprises but they could not buy the shares. They could not sell the business, nor could they seek foreign partners. The system became stuck in a sea of decision-making, and contributed to the rise of a new bureaucracy where management ran the enterprises like their own kingdoms.

The government could have evaluated the assets of its 300 000 enterprises, but this would have taken much longer. Instead, it intended to implement privatisation from below. To do this, it will issue coupons to those employees wishing to obtain shares in their companies. Employees must buy the shares, which will be available at a discount rate ranging from 30 to 70 per cent. For every year of employment, employees will have the right to a discount of 1 per cent. A discount of 30 per cent will automatically be given to the workforce at the start of privatisation. The money from the sale will not be channelled back into the enterprise. Instead, it goes to a Development Fund which was set up in April 1990 with the task of accumulating resources and capital.

Opposition to the proposals is considerable from the republics. Slovenia wants to transform socially-owned property into state property, and it wants to break away from the central government. Croatia's freely elected right-wing parliament aims to bring the socially-owned enterprises under state control before it introduces privatisation, thereby replacing one clan of government chiefs with another. In Serbia, resistance to privatisation has been the toughest. In one instance, workers voted to privatise their factory, but the decision was blocked by the courts in Belgrade, the federal and republic capital of Serbia. In common with other Eastern bloc countries, opposition also comes from the management.

The Yugoslavian media is so fragmented that it is difficult to educate the people on the merits of privatisation. Republics which don't agree with the reforms are also banning speeches about them in their media.

6

AFRICA

In Africa, privatisation has been popular through management contracts and leasing. For example, the Ivory Coast has contracted out its water supply network and Kenya has tendered its road construction and maintenance.

Egypt

Public sector investment makes up three-quarters of total Egyptian investment spending. In its latest five-year plan (1987–92) the government plans to help its nationalised projects to privatise. There are over two hundred and fifty such projects operating on a commercial basis, most of them engaged in poultry, fish, animal feed, meat and dairy products. Tourism, agriculture and supermarkets are targeted as potential privatisation prospects. Already, the Ministry of Tourism has privatised almost all of its eighteen hotels.

Morocco

The Moroccan Government has also adopted privatisation plans and recently adopted legislation to privatise 113 enterprises, including four leading banks and thirty-seven hotels, within six years. This will be carried out through tendering, transference through the financial market, or a combination of both. Enterprises to be privatised will not include strategic sectors such as the important phosphate industry, the national airline, the central bank, the railways, or water and electricity utilities.

Nigeria

The Nigerian Government is selling its stake in hundreds of companies. The official mandate to privatise dates from the early 1980s. By June 1990, the state had divested most large public utilities, the petrol and mining authorities, telecommunications, electric power, and a steel company, retaining a share in some. The National Bank of Nigeria and the National Oil and Chemical Marketing Company Ltd were sold by public offering. In cases where the government's share was too small for a public offering shares were offered to the firm's employees. Problems included a lack of credit which hindered sales. The government had to encourage banks to lend. By 1990, the Technical Committee on Privatisation and Commercialisation had sold over fifty-six million shares with a market capitalization of eighty-nine million naira. It also has a public offering of over forty million shares for small and medium-sized insurance companies.

South Africa

The South African Government has tried to limit its participation in the economy. Sasol, an oil-from-coal company, was privatised in 1979. At that point it was the biggest listing on the Johannesburg Stock Exchange with over twenty-six thousand shareholders. By 1985, public sector expenditure amounted to 38.1 per cent of the gross domestic product. The result of the growth in public sector spending meant that only limited capital was available for investment in the private sector. Investment was also impeded by compulsory investment in loan funds that had to be provided to finance public corporations and state business enterprises. A White Paper on privatisation was presented to the president in November 1986. The paper pointed out that the growth of spending in the public sector had:

- decreased the private sector's share and thus its tax base in the economy;

- made higher taxation levels necessary;

- caused a situation in which the public sector was unable to cover its current expenditure from current revenue;

- decreased the public sector contribution to net domestic saving between 1981 and 1985;

- weakened the capital/output ratio in South Africa;

- contributed to high inflation.

The 1985 debt crisis had added to the impetus. Foreign banks had refused to roll-over the country's debt. Until then the country had relied on capital for fixed investment coming from abroad.

President Botha announced the programme in February 1988 with only five big candidates. These were the Electricity Supply Commission, the Iron and Steel Corporation (ISCOR), the South African Transport Services, the Phosphate Development Corporation (Foskor), and Posts and Telecommunications. In 1989, these companies had assets of R73 billion.

The African National Congress (ANC) and other organisations on the left are opposed to the programme. They believe that the privatisation will frustrate their plans for redistribution under a non-racial regime. In response the government has agreed to channel over £220 million of future privatisation proceeds into 'social upliftment' projects.

The government believes that privatisation should form part of a deal consisting of economic reform measures which are directed towards a healthy business climate. In response to black pressure, the government also agreed to privatise Sorghum Beer, which is drunk mainly by blacks, by handing it to black entrepreneurs who will understand how to market it.

ISCOR was listed in November 1989. It was 4.16 times oversubscribed and encouraged over 150 000 investors to come to the market. After reaching a high in the following January, the share slumped back to its issue price, largely because earnings forecasts were unlikely to be met. Iscor ran into two problems: world steel prices softened in the second half of the year, and one of its furnaces broke down, which cost over 250,000 tonnes in export sales. By the following November, ISCOR's first set of annual results showed that its share price had fallen 10 cents below the listing price of 200 South African cents. This, combined with continued opposition from the ANC and an absence of suitable candidates for privatisation, has put the programme largely on the back burner.

The company's post-privatisation strategy is now focusing on shifting production towards higher-value-added products. ISCOR is now converting from profile to flat-type products at Pretoria and increasing its capacity at the hot steel mill in another area so that higher-value slabs can be produced. With the abolition of apartheid, the company is also hoping to look to expansion in the internal market and to the lifting of American and European Community sanctions.

The South African Transport Network (Transnet) recently took a step towards privatisation by restructuring. It has divided into five business units and changed its status from state corporation to private company. The Electricity Supply Commission has been building the basis for competitive operation for some years now, but its sale has been put back because it has little competition. However, as one commentator put it, 'Privatisation is the crowning of the commercialisation process. You can defer the coronation so long as you get on with the commercialisation process.'

Togo

A Ministry of Industry and State Enterprises was established in 1984 to monitor and reform state enterprises. Leasing to foreign companies has proved a popular option following political difficulties with the outright sale of assets. The Société Togolaise de Siderurgie was leased in 1984 to an American for 20 years. Since the handover, the company has been running at a profit. A Danish company has leased Soprolait, a dairy farming company. Other foreign companies have bought hefty shares in Togo's denationalised companies. For example, Société Togolaise des Hydrocarbures, a government-owned oil refinery and storage facility, was leased to Shell International which later took a 60 per cent share. The state still holds 40 per cent of the equity in the firm, renamed Compel.

Tunisia

Tunisia has a ratio of public to private ownership of approximately 60/40. According to the Centre for Privatisation, it is moving rapidly through a programme of privatisation. Reasons for the programme's success, according to the Centre, include the government's commitment to the programme, the use of one, powerful privatisation committee located in the prime minister's office, collaboration with the World Bank and USAID, and the government's acceptance of technical assistance from the centre's experts.

Bibliography

Butler, Eammon, Director of the Adam Smith Institute, editor, Privatisation in practice, ASI Research Ltd, 1988

Chapman, Colin, *Selling the Family Silver*, Hutchinson Business Books, London, November 1990

Centre for Privatisation, 'Privatisation Survey for Developing Countries', March 1990

Evans, Richard, 'Privatisation verdict awaited', *Financial Times*, March 11, 1991

Leadbeater, Charles, Thomas, David, and Betts, Paul, 'Private Lives and Public Problems', *Financial Times*, December 8 1990

Leadbeater, Charles, 'Political debate too simplistic', *Financial Times*, August 8 1990

Pirie, Dr Madsen, President of the Adam Smith Institute, Privatisation, Wildwood House, Aldershot, 1988

White Paper on Privatisation and Deregulation in the Republic of South Africa

Vickers, John and Wright, Vincent, *The Politics of Privatisation in Western Europe*, Frank Cass and Company, London, 1989 pp 6–9

Wright, Mike, Robbie, Ken, and Thompson, Steve, 'The Role of Management Buy-outs in Privatisation: an international perspective', CMBOR Occasional Paper 18, CMBOR (The Centre for Management Buy-out Research)

Young, David, 'Privatised sector shines in list of profits and pay', *The Times*, March 27, 1990

Part II
CASE STUDIES

1

BRITISH TELECOM

Iain Vallance
Chairman, British Telecommunications plc

Some seven years after the contentious but outstandingly successful privatisation and flotation which media commentators dubbed the 'Sale of the Century', and which paved the way for the even larger public share offers that followed, British Telecom stands at another crucial point on its development path as we restructure our business to meet the communications challenges and opportunities of the next decade — and especially to focus more sharply upon our customers and their changing needs.

As a privatised public limited company operating in a highly competitive market, our overall performance record since mid-1984 has already been one of considerable achievement, particularly in terms of the greatly improved quality of service and value for money which we now offer to our twenty million domestic and five and a half million business customers. I am convinced that we would not have achieved anything near as much for our customers had we still been in the state sector, of which we were a significant element, and the near-monopoly service provider, for over seventy years.

Yet only a few years into our life as a plc we already find ourselves facing another prolonged testing period, played out like our privatisation in the full glare of media, political and public attention, as the government undertakes the first major formal review of UK telecommunications competition and related communications issues — a process whose outcome will determine the way ahead for our industry, and for all customers and users, into the twenty-first century.

As this crucial review gets under way, and as we press on in the meantime with the strategies and initiatives which are taking us steadily towards our declared vision of becoming the most successful worldwide telecommunications company, we also find ourselves the subject of much continuing speculation as to whether the present government may offer all or some of its residual shareholding in British Telecom for sale this side of the next general election, or afterwards should it be returned to power. There has been much continuing speculation, too, that British Telecom could be taken back into some form of state ownership or majority control, should that election result in a Labour victory and subsequent implementation of the present opposition's declared policy.

These are, of course, wholly and solely matters for the government of the day, not for ourselves, to decide, as were the policy decisions and legislative programmes which led up to our privatisation and flotation. But British Telecom's attitude towards a possible further share sale is clear and on record. Even today, after the celebrated public offer in November 1984 and the subsequent allocation of several further parcels of shares to cover British Telecom staff profits-related and share-saving schemes, the Government still owns 48.8 per cent of our company — almost as much as all our other private and institutional shareholders combined. Should it choose to divest itself of some or all of that holding, then our remaining shackles and ties with the bad old state sector and government department years would be diminished or even totally severed. That, we feel, would be no bad thing.

Our British Telecom view of the prospect of renewed state ownership or control is equally clear. Experience of operating in both the public and private sector environments, and the contrasts and comparisons we are now able to draw, have convinced us beyond all doubt that it is as a privatised competitive company, and not as an arm of the state at the constant mercy of political influence and intervention, that we are best placed to serve our customers and the country well, now and in the foreseeable future.

Since 1984, we have always remained very mindful of the fact that our privatisation and flotation should not be taken as an assumption of remaining a public limited company for all time. If we were to revert to state ownership or control, such a dramatic change would impact greatly not only upon British Telecom, but also upon all the millions of private share-holders who have invested in us and in the other privatised service industries — and in our seventh year in the private sector we still command the loyalty of some 1.2 million shareholders, the vast majority of them individuals, spread throughout Britain, as well as overseas. Their support, to-gether with that of the majority of our staff who also form a substantial element of British Telecom shareholders, must, we feel, reflect some significant measure of satisfaction with our performance and our current status.

Looking back even less than ten years, to the time when Telecommunications was still part of the old Post Of-fice — and when 'subscribers', as they were often then still called, could have any telephone they wanted from the monopoly provider, as long as it was black or grey and rented, and they did not want one too quickly — it is now hard to remember those difficult years when we were subject to what even one of our sponsoring ministers described in Parliament in the run-up to our privatisation as 'a web of interference and control'.

The scenario through the 1980s, which began with British Telecom's separation and creation as a self-contained state sector corporation, against a background of rapid technolo-gical change in all aspects of telecommunications, very much reinforces our view that privatisation was just one step, albeit a most important and timely one, in our evolutionary progress.

Closely allied to privatisation, yet running shortly ahead of it in the Government's legislative timetable, had come liberalisation — or competition, as it is more popularly called. Throughout the past decade, these two fundamental departures from previous UK telecommunications practice were closely and inextricably linked. It was their powerful combined impact which began to produce the radical market changes and wide freedom of choice which have been so beneficial to all our customers.

I feel I cannot better the words of our then Secretary of State for Trade and Industry, Nicholas Ridley MP, who in June 1990 so neatly and aptly summarised the rapid transformation of UK telecommunications achieved in the 1980s as a 'wonder of the world'. Reminding an audience of businessmen of the type of consumer problems commonplace in many of the state sector service industries a few years earlier, he declared: 'We privatised British Telecom and freed the market-place, and now the UK communications industry has become a wonder of the world in a decade.' For anyone to seek to reverse that process, Mr Ridley added, would be to fly in the face of everything that had been achieved under the liberalisation policy and 'to go back to the economics of the German Democratic Republic.'

When British Telecom formally became a public limited company in August 1984 and had just over half of its newly-created shares floated in London and New York less than four months later, the sales represented not only the largest and most ambitious single offer so far attempted by Mrs Thatcher's government, but also the beginning of a determined bid to revive private investment in Britain.

The flotation of British Telecom broke all Stock Exchange statistical records at that time as the largest public offering ever made, and assured us of a permanent place in the record books. Moreover, it succeeded in capturing and retaining the attention of millions of people who, although already familiar with British Telecom as customers and users of our services, had never in their wildest dreams thought of themselves as participants in the world of finance and equities. Yet, at the end of what was by any standards a unique marketing and public relations operation — one which has already spawned a classic case-study textbook for marketing students — some 2.3 million people throughout Britain, as well as all the expected institutional investors, had put in bids and become founder shareholders in our company. We also achieved by far the biggest take-up of shares by any company workforce at that time, with almost 96 per cent of our eligible 238 000 employees accepting their allocations of free shares and almost 80 per cent putting in their own money to acquire a direct financial interest in the well-being of the company that employed them.

The 'Sale of the Century', as it had been called beforehand, suddenly then became the sales success of the century, in terms of both quantity and quality. It pioneered the new mass shareholder movement and smoothed the way for the successful sales of other major state industries as part of the government's ongoing denationalisation programme, notably British Gas and British Airways, who were able to learn from our British Telecom experience and build upon our solid foundation.

The final verdict came on 3 December 1984, when I and my board colleagues made the short journey from our City of London company headquarters to the Stock Exchange for the real acid test of success — the simultaneous official start of trading in our shares in London and on Wall Street.

The colourful scene which greeted us on the trading floor of the Exchange, appropriately bedecked for the occasion with giant telephones and our company logo, was one of hectic and eager anticipation. As soon as dealing began, we knew that the government's and our own ambitions had been fully realised. It was an occasion for discreet celebration and satisfaction, particularly for my predecessor as chairman, Sir George Jefferson, and for our then deputy chairman, Deryk Van der Weyer, who had joined us full-time from Barclays Bank to help steer us through the most eventful single step in our history.

The success of British Telecom's privatisation and flotation was not achieved without a great deal of hard and intensive work by a great many people of disparate interests and backgrounds, working together as a team to a demanding time-scale. Yet as we witnessed the beginning of trading in London, and heard the equally good news from New York, we took most satisfaction and comfort from the fact that, despite all the additional burdens and demands which privatisation and flotation had inevitably placed upon British Telecom — even though government was the instigator and seller — we had got on, as ever, behind the scenes with the primary task of trying to serve and satisfy our then twenty million customers. Our undivided managerial attention could now be directed back to this relentless task — and to beginning to try to live up to most, if not all, of the hopes, expectations and promises which had been nurtured among our new army of shareholders and the British and overseas publics at large during the marketing and flotation period.

For the first time, British Telecom was in the business of serving and satisfying shareholders as well as customers, of working to earn and retain their continued loyalty and financial support through our performance and achievements. Despite our new commercial freedom, we knew that the immediate future would not be easy. We knew that we still had quite some way to go to even catch up with the legacies of the past which had left us with a telecommunications network which, although already one of Europe's and the world's largest, was far from modern or capable of supporting all the services and products our customers were increasingly demanding from us.

We certainly had some sales success to live up to, judging by the media verdicts. For once, the commentators were unanimous. The *Sun* hailed it as 'a brilliant success'. *The Financial Times* called it 'a monumental corporate finance exercise and, in almost every respect, a monumental achievement', while the *Daily Mail* declared: 'Never has there been such a city launch. Never has there been such a stampede to buy shares.'

The Daily Telegraph's conclusion was: 'The biggest, best publicised and most highly stage-managed share sale in history was put to the test in the marketplace yesterday and received with rapturous approval.' Even the harder-headed regional press, less used to being caught up in such City euphoria, joined in the accolades: 'The scale of this privatisation success surpasses every expectation,' said *The Yorkshire Post.*

How had we reached this milestone in world telecommunications, as the first major public operator ever to be privatised in this way — and what lay ahead of our customers as we and they began to encounter the first real effects of competition?

The years since I joined the then General Post Office in 1966 had been ones of accelerating growth, change and diversification as telecommunications began to encompass more than simple telephone and telex services, and to exert increasing influence upon the nation's industrial, commercial and social life. It soon became apparent to me that this capital-intensive business was beginning to demand more and more of the precious national financial resources to meet growing customer expectations — and that it was becoming increasingly unrealistic for a government-run monopoly, competing against all the other demands upon the limited public purse, to be able to satisfy every need, especially in the business customer sector. Official recognition of this situation came in October 1969, when we ceased to be a government department and became a state industry managed for the first time by a chairman and board — but still answerable to a government minister and still a business within the overall Post Office umbrella.

The 1970s were years when the pressures for UK change became almost irresistible, mirroring the significant technological progress and market changes beginning to impact upon our industry throughout the developed world. In 1979 came a change of government, and it was largely in response to this great movement for change, for which many customers were by now clamouring, that the 1981 Act of Parliament finally established us as a business in our own right, made provision for a steady build-up of market competition (including the licensing of a second UK public network operator) and laid the framework for licensing new competitive value-added services like electronic mail and mobile communications which have provided so much of the spectacular UK market growth in recent years.

Three years later — not as early as the government had planned, because of the intervention of the 1983 general election — came the 1984 Telecommunications Act which eliminated further vestiges of our old monopoly rights, created the new Office of Telecommunications under a full-time director general to enforce licences governing all UK operators and providers, transferred our British Telecom assets to the new plc — and set the scene for floating 'the people's share', as it quickly became known.

Privatisation and liberalisation were a natural corollary. The government had signalled its intention to open up almost the entire UK market to competition, promoting new services and products and customer choice. I doubt if a monolithic, nationalised business like ours could have adapted itself to such an environment, given that the government was determined to push through market competition even faster than it was being achieved in the United States through the break-up of the Bell conglomerate.

We were certainly not well placed at that time to respond speedily and flexibly to customer needs, even as a monopoly, and our new competitors would have been deeply suspicious of such a major publicly-funded player in the market-place. If British Telecom was to compete fully and fairly in the new environment it seemed only right that we should also compete on our own ability for the private capital we needed to finance the growth and modernisation which were long overdue. Here was both a challenge and the great opportunity we needed to rid our business of so many outdated customs and practices, to focus upon the needs of our customers, rather than upon our own internal administrative convenience, to enter new home and overseas markets, and to take full advantage of the many varying demands for what we could offer, now that we had the promise of greater freedom to do so.

Up to 1980 our business had continued in much the same kind of organisational and traditional way as it had ever since the old GPO became responsible for almost all UK public telephone services in 1912 — although, paradoxically, these had been the subject of intense uncontrolled competition in some parts of the country since before the GPO established its own first exchanges in 1881. Between 1980, when the British Telecom trading name first appeared, and 1984 we began the enormous task of changing the old three-tier centralised structure and committee style of management. We had to be ready to meet the twin challenges of competition, which began with the simple supply of extension telephones, and of the privatisation which lay ahead, even though we remained wholly in the state sector for the time being.

Devolution and decentralisation were very much the watchwords, as we sought to eliminate our middle tier of regional administration, to push decision-making and managerial responsibility down the line, and to give our field managers full control over, and accountability for, all the financial, engineering, technical and human resources which they so desperately needed, within a cohesive national framework, to do the best possible job for their customers.

By November 1982, amid much contention, controversy and opposition, not least from our own staff unions, the government had brought its British Telecom privatisation Bill into the Commons — by which time our key competitor had already received its first operating licence and begun to plan its own business strategies and networks, which, unlike our own, could be created from scratch using the most modern exchange switching and transmission techniques. Nevertheless, much of the future shape of network competiton would depend upon the integration and interconnection of the two systems and upon the commercial terms of that interconnection.

By May 1983, after completing all its fiercely contested clause-by-clause Committee stages in both Houses, the Bill was not far short of receiving the Royal Assent when it automatically fell with the dissolution of Parliament and the calling of a June election. The government was returned, but we were literally back in the hands of the Parliamentary draughtsmen, since an entirely new Bill was necessary to achieve the original privatisation objective. That gave us in British Telecom some more unexpected time to continue our reshaping, but the experience had not been without some benefits, since many valuable lessons learned from the passage of the original Bill were carried into its successor. The new Bill came into the Commons exactly a year after the first — and, amid continuing controversy, went through all its stages and received formal Royal Assent on 12 July 1984. At last, the way ahead was clear.

Our intensive behind-the-scenes preparations had involved not only much work within British Telecom, but also the complicated multi-faceted negotiations with government and its advisers which helped to determine the shape of the legislation, the content of the new long-term operating licences so crucial to our commercial and competitive future, and, of course, the sort of price at which the newly-created nominal 25p shares might be sold. All of these negotiations broke entirely new ground for all parties. At the same time, we also had to bring our accounting up to the commercial requirements of a plc and of company law, and negotiate an entirely new capital structure for our business with government. Finally, we needed to create the formal comprehensive prospectus which would enable one of Britain's biggest businesses to be floated and its shares sold simultaneously in Europe, North America and Japan in a way that fulfilled the regulatory requirements of all markets to the letter.

Much of the internal and external work was of a pioneering nature. When the joint marketing committee, charged with the task of planning and sustaining the environment for a successful sale, met for the first time in our boardroom in July 1983, its members faced a daunting task — to create interest in British Telecom shares not only among the institutions, but on an unprecedented scale among a public with little recent involvement in equities, and of whom under 1.8 million then owned shares of any kind. The problem facing the team, drawn from the government's two merchant banks, its two principal stockbrokers, its civil servants from the Department of Trade and Industry and the Treasury, and from our own senior executives, was clear. The solutions, at that stage, were far from apparent.

There were no precedents to help mould either the marketing or public relations strategies and programmes. Every decision seemed to be a trail-blazer and had to satisfy so many other parties — lawyers, other bankers and brokers, the marketing, public relations and advertising specialists, as well as government, ourselves and our own British Telecom advisers. Those meetings of the main and sub-working groups merged the cultures and requirements of occasionally almost incompatible interests into a force which was to achieve one of the greatest marketing conditioning achievements on record.

The main committee created the pre-sale policy and programmes. Throughout the advance campaign, it monitored every action and approved every initiative from whatever source. Much reliance was placed upon continuous and comprehensive market research as a key indicator of public attitudes and possible buying intentions. A significant early factor to emerge was the standing in the community of our own employees.

We had already made many advances in bringing in senior managers experienced in private industry to combine with the best of our own people. We had made many advances in improving our service and the quality and range of our products. The waiting list for basic telephone service, which had peaked at over a quarter of a million, had been largely eradicated. New exchanges were entering service daily. We were bringing in new optical fibre cables in place of some of the traditional copper cables, and speeding up the modernisation of our main networks as far as capital investment allowed. New services for business customers were being introduced. But the rolling attitudinal research, which had begun some years before privatisation, still showed little upward improvement in customer perception, highlighting the critical need to put over stronger, sustained messages about the new British Telecom. Out of this work came our 'Power Behind the Button' campaign, which began in November 1983, to secure recognition of our achievements and prospects, and of a growing role in the community beyond our mainstream service business.

Coinciding with this advance public campaign, and running in tandem with it, came a whole raft of British Telecom-organised activities aimed particularly at the media, MPs, major customers, other key opinion formers and our own staff. For example, we staged our first week-long exhibition in the Guildhall in the City of London, using it as a backdrop to brief the bankers, brokers and specialist telecommunications industry analysts whose support would be crucial to a successful share offer. Another exhibition was at our Martlesham research laboratories near Ipswich, where we staged an exciting combination of current products and the technology behind those of the future. We stepped up our presence and identity at the major world exhibition and technical forum staged every four years in Geneva. Between these three events, we did £12 million worth of business — even though they had not been conceived as selling occasions! We also revived what we now called Telecom Focus, a nationwide programme of visits and events at our operational buildings to show ourselves at work to our customers.

Another vital strand of our own British Telecom activity was to counter the real concerns being created among our customers by internal opposition to denationalisation. This was, in itself, a difficult and prolonged exercise, devised and

executed to increase staff understanding by providing a flow
of information about what we considered to be the inevitabil-
ity of privatisation.

One further crucial decision was the choice of message to
underpin our main corporate advertising campaign at that
stage. It was that 'You too can share in British Telecom's
future' — and despite the handicaps of advertising in advance
an unknown and untested product without a price tag, we
created a campaign which captured the interest of the nation.

At a very early stage, it was decided that the physical focus
for the selling campaign should be our own British Telecom
technology. The 'golden' 0272 272 272 telephone number,
plus a simple box number address, directed the bulk of
enquiries from potential investors to our own Bristol-based
telemarketing operation, which provided telephone and cou-
pon response mechanisms for our customers' promotional
campaigns. In a little over three months, that unit processed
almost 1.4 million requests for more information, a record at
that time, responding with a combination of leaflets and
publications whose production and logistical management
was a Herculean task in itself. A specially prepared layman's
guide to buying and selling shares, as well as the actual
preliminary prospectus, were also essential ingredients of the
response, since the government was aiming to spread our
shares as widely as possible, and to raise more money than the
institutions were then investing in all shares over the course of
a year. This sum of funds within their control underlined the
vast scale of what was now being attempted.

The institutional programme itself was innovative. For
example, a travelling train, based on our established product
and services sales train, toured the country in June and July
1984, making presentations to financial intermediaries to
ensure that they also had the best possible understanding of
British Telecom and of the scale of the actual issue. A
roadshow nearer the time reinforced our earlier messages and
took two teams to overseas audiences in seven countries. 'I've

never seen anything like it. For once, it looks that you've got something to teach us,' was one North American banker's reaction.

As the government's selling campaign entered its critical phase, when it was essential to ensure perceptions of British Telecom were based solely on the prospectus, this constraint, applying to any company seeking a Stock Exchange listing, became particularly taxing for one of our size and complexity — and one almost permanently in the public eye. The set-piece launch of the pathfinder prospectus, containing everything bar the actual offer price, was the one and only remaining chance for the media to get their stories and put their questions to the principal players. The occasion was played out under the full glare of television coverage. All the signs were promising as enquiries to Bristol peaked to thirty thousand a day.

Three weeks later came the issue of the full prospectus and announcement of the all-important 130p total price tag, with shares to be subscribed for through an initial 50p offer, then subsequently to be paid for by successful applicants with two further phased payments of 40p per share. Some 42.5 million items of film and print, not including the final prospectuses, had been issued in the course of all the campaigns. The newspaper prospectus and application form ran to ten consecutive broadsheet pages, a media record.

The response was in line with the final highest expectations predicted by the research. When applications closed on 28 November, the issue of 3012 million shares had been almost five times oversubscribed and the wider share-ownership breakthrough had been achieved. 'Massive oversubscription', 'Millions of first-time buyers', ran the confident and accurate press headlines.

In retrospect, our flotation came to be seen as a classic operation on a scale that guaranteed us a permanent place in the record books. Now, we in British Telecom had to deliver in terms of service and performance, as well as profitability. Early in our determined efforts to confound our critics came another significant stage in market liberalisation, as the end of 1984 saw the abolition of our continued monopoly right to provide the first instrument attached to any telephone line. All our customers, domestic and business, now had the full freedom of choice of telephone supplier and the freedom to buy, rather than rent. A revolution in UK telecommunications had truly begun.

Today, despite some setbacks along the way, notably our well-chronicled difficulties of 1987 which found service and customer satisfaction at a low ebb, I believe we can look back on a catalogue of British Telecom achievements which confirm our ability to compete successfully in the world's most highly liberalised market and which have benefited all our customers.

Our recent performance, in terms of the service we offer, our investment for the future and profitablility for our shareholders, is back at record levels and there are many tangible measures of our turnaround. In 1984, before privatisation, we had just one modern digital exchange in operation. Now, our entire national network operates digitally, the first of its size anywhere in the world to do so. We have almost three thousand local modern exchanges serving some eleven million customers. Then, we had only thirteen thousand kilometres of optical fibre cable in service. Now, we have more than a million kilometres, a higher proportion than any comparable telephone company. Before, we had no itemised billing capability. Now, this option is available to half of all our customers.

In 1984, we had a neglected, unmodernised Directory Enquiry Service largely dependent upon books and paper records. Today, it is fully computerised and more speedily and cost-effectively handling unprecedented workloads after investment of some £140 million. We had a run-down, much criticised public payphone service. Now, after investment of £160 million, we have over ninety thousand new ones, mostly in new-style housings, with at least 95 per cent working at any time, offering a variety of payment facilities. In 1984, our old mobile telephone service had yet to be superseded by new cellular technology. Today, our Cellnet network covers most of the country and caters, in full competition, for almost half a million users.

There was then no compatible computerised customer service system — our records were spread round several limited facilities. Now, our 'front office' system is in place throughout the country, making it easier for us to respond efficiently and flexibly to customer needs. Before privatisation, with service provided under general schemes rather than specific contracts, there was little or no consumer protection. Now, our service is provided to contract, and our Customer Guarantee Scheme covering speed of provision and repairs has become the model for other service industries to match.

We have achieved these milestones over a period in which, by July 1990, the prices of our regulated basket of main inland telephone services had already fallen in real purchasing power terms by almost a quarter since privatisation, measured against the government's retail price index.

In 1984, we were also predominantly a domestic company, with few overseas business activities other than consultancy services. We have since made a number of key investments overseas, notably in the fields of electronic mail, data networks and cellular telephony, in line with our strategy of pursuing relevant market opportunities outside Britain — something we would never have been allowed to do in our former state sector years. Yet the bulk of our capital investment, and the foundation of our determination to become a world-class player, remains in our commitment to the UK and to providing world-class network services and related facilities to our UK customers.

So many of our past problems and inadequacies could be traced back to the years when we were constantly held back by constraints on our borrowing limits and our essential capital spending programme. In 1989–90, we invested a record £3115 million in modernisation and growth, more than double our pre-privatisation investment level.

During the 1990s, as we look forward, among other things, to the implementation of the Single European Market and to inevitable liberalisation and change in other telecommunications markets, we expect to see any number of new opportunities for generating extra earnings growth — provided that we choose and understand our markets well and succeed in putting customers first. We shall aim to defend our UK market base from increasing competition, much of it from major international companies. We shall attack our chosen markets overseas, concentrating upon those areas where we have demonstrated a successful track record and upon providing our customers with total solutions to their communications problems.

The major reshaping of British Telecom we are now carrying through, from a position of strength, reflects the still changing nature of the market-place, as domestic and international boundaries become less important and the competition for major customers worldwide becomes far more intense. So, we have to sharpen up to stay ahead. Project Sovereign is enabling us to focus much faster and more sharply on widely differing needs, to take decisions on them more quickly and cost-effectively, and to satisfy them in a fast, flexible and quality way. We will emerge as a leaner, more supple organisation, while remaining the only UK operator obliged to provide a universal service which meets all reasonable customer demands.

Yet we still need to cater as a privatised public service operator for those external factors over which we have little or no control. The nature and extent of regulation over our activities, and the relationship between regulation and competition, remains the most important of these. That is why the first post-privatisation, competition policy review is of such importance to us and to all telecommunications users.

Free and vigorous competition is demonstrably the best way for users to get real service and value for money. But true and fair competition cannot take place here in Britain unless the continuing distortion in our British Telecom pricing structure can be rectified. If this anomaly is recognised and sensitively handled in the government's review, then there will be good prospects of genuine UK competition. As competition increases, regulation must diminish. This was very much the medium-term intention when British Telecom was privatised, although it was understandable to tilt the playing field in favour of our competitors through their market entry phases. A reduction in regulation is in the best interests of our British Telecom customers overall and of our shareholders.

Since our privatisation, and especially since 1987, we believe we have made substantial progress towards our ultimate goal of becoming a successful company in world terms. We now need a period of stability to enable us to see through the programmes we have begun for the benefit of our customers. None of us in British Telecom wants to experience a return to the times when we were so very much a political football, at the mercy of stop-start pricing, investment and planning policies which characterised our state sector era. Under our present status, we have the opportunity to consolidate our progress and build upon the initiatives which have transformed British Telecom and created, through our own and other privatisations, a new share-owning democracy.

2

SEAT

This study has been prepared by Jose Maria Viedma, Professor of Management at Cataluña Polytechnical University (UPC), and translated by Paul Gould. The information used as a basis for this study was supplied by SEAT.

Spain produced some of the first cars of international repute, such as the Hispano Suiza and the Pegaso, individually built by craftsmen just as the Rolls-Royce is today. The first serious attempt to establish a modern car industry in Spain, capable of mass production, was the creation of SEAT in 1950, with the state as the major shareholder in the company.

In post-war Spain, at a time when there was no auxiliary industry and no specialised workforce, SEAT managed to start up a modern enterprise, which in its turn created hundreds of auxiliary businesses to supply technical accessories, patents and even capital — and all in under two years. It was this initial effort by SEAT which made it possible, years later, for American and other European car manufacturers to set up factories in Spain for the production of their own cars. In this way, SEAT has not only produced seven million cars of its own, but has also indirectly made it possible for a further ten million cars to be manufactured in Spain since 1950.

SEAT was born in the socio-economic climate of Spain in the early 1950s, at the suggestion of the National Institute of

Industry, Spain's public industrial development body. An agreement was signed with the Italian manufacturer Fiat, which also supplied the technology, but the Spanish state was the major shareholder.

The birth of SEAT must be understood within the context of the social, political and economic situation in Spain during the 1940s and 1950s. The country had lived under a totalitarian regime, without pluralist or democratic institutions, and in spite of not having taken an active part in the Second World War now found itself on the side of the losers. This meant that Spain was not only isolated from other Western and European nations, but also that she was unable to receive aid for industrial reconstruction.

SEAT brought mass production to Spain, using industrial processes and assembly lines. At the same time, it was the pioneer in the creation of a large-scale automotive industry: these days Spain is the fourth largest car manufacturer in Europe. That first venture, set up in 1950, started making and selling cars in 1953, and significantly boosted the social and economic development of a country where pockets of under-development still existed. SEAT helped to transform Spain in more ways than one: on the one hand, a large number of people and their families moved from the country to the city (to Barcelona and its outskirts), attracted by jobs in industry. Some of these jobs were indirectly connected with SEAT, working in supply industries which had grown up around the car company. Secondly, thanks to mass production, SEAT helped to make the motor car available to the man in the street, especially from 1957 onwards after the launch of the popular 600 model. Once the car became widespread and began to travel, much-needed road improvements rapidly came throughout Spain.

The first thirty years of SEAT's existence were years of uninterrupted success, with new models and a steady annual increase in production; and all this while still state-owned.

Were it not for the nature of being a state-owned enterprise, certain episodes in SEAT's development would be hard to understand or appreciate. The most relevant example is when SEAT had to take over both the plant and the workforce of AUTHI, after the Pamplona-based company stopped producing Morris cars in Spain.

In 1980, as a result of the effects of the oil crisis, Fiat — who had previously claimed to have total control over SEAT during the privatisation process — decided to abandon the whole project and gave up its stake in the Spanish firm. This meant that almost all of SEAT's diminished capital became the property of the INI (National Industry Institute).

SEAT's problems at this time can be summarised as follows:

- overmanning;

- lack of its own technology;

- no external sales network;

- decreasing sales.

The Spanish company had to overcome this difficult period alone, abandoned by its former partner. It was a period in which two stages can be discerned. The first, from 1980 to 1983, saw SEAT launch its own models and establish a market outside Spain which had not previously existed. The second stage saw the securing of a strategic deal via a merger with Volkswagen, one of the world's largest car manufacturers, to produce the German firm's Passat, Santana and Polo models in SEAT plants. This meant that SEAT's established industrial capacity was used to the full. Additionally, as part of the deal, SEAT gained exclusive rights to import and sell Volkswagen and Audi cars in Spain. These deals were very relevant at the time, since they must be seen in the light of the changes that had necessarily taken place in the Spanish market: Spain had just joined the European Community and had thus started to abolish protectionist trade barriers.

The absorption of SEAT by Volkswagen was the result of recognising mutual benefits for both companies: The benefits for SEAT were:

- Fulfilling the 1981–85 plan of action which aimed to:
  - reduce the staffing levels;
  - produce SEAT's own models;
  - create a sales network abroad.

- Finding an international partner who would provide:
  - competition on an international level;
  - technology;
  - savings in the size of the operation;
  - additional sales;
  - a way to make the best use of existing manufacturing facilities.

- The benefits for Volkswagen were:
  - penetrating the Spanish market;
  - consolidating its position as market leader in Europe;
  - increasing competitiveness and productivity.

The integration of SEAT into Volkswagen took place gradually, enabling both sides to get to know each other. This gradual development has been an important factor in determining the outcome of the merger; the two sides trod carefully, checking that the ground was firm before each stage:

September 1985	: Deal made, outlining technical and commercial co-operation.
June 1986	: Volkswagen acquired 51 per cent of SEAT.
December 1986	: Volkswagen increased its stake in SEAT to 75 per cent.

By 31 December 1990 : Volkswagen to own 100 per
cent of SEAT's capital.

Thanks to the signing of these deals, SEAT was able to
consolidate its standing as a marque, recover from the effects
of being abandoned by Fiat, and use its own factories and
workforce to the full. At the same time, it opened up the
Spanish market for Volkswagen which now, instead of the
merely symbolic presence it had previously had, sold more
cars in Spain than in any country apart from Germany.

With hindsight, the agreement can only be understood
against the economic backdrop of the time. An independent
SEAT which maintained its status as a state enterprise was not
viable within the context of the European Community. For
Volkswagen, the experience gained between 1983 and 1986
had shown that acquiring SEAT was a strategic opportunity.
Thus, after the relevant negotiations, SEAT became a member
of the German consortium, contributing to its lead in Europe
by selling SEAT cars in newly-opened areas of the market.

In order to keep up with the requirements of the agreement,
the company needed new capital and a restructured workforce. SEAT not only suffered from overmanning, but also
from having an excessively old employee age profile; most
employees had been with the company since its very first
years of existence. The flexibility of the Spanish labour market
meant that all firms, and especially SEAT, had had to run for
decades without any real choice when it came to recruitment.
The worst effects of this were that most Spanish firms suffered
from a sharp downturn in productivity, and that many of these
were not able to install new technology in time. Consequently
SEAT's prime objectives were to refit its factories and to
employ a younger staff. This they managed to do humanely, by
offering workers the possibility of early retirement and redundancy incentives, and taking on young skilled workers.

The main changes which privatisation has brought to SEAT
are largely thanks to a new style of management and a new

organisational structure. On becoming part of the Volkswagen-Audi Group, SEAT's organisational structure started to resemble that of Volkswagen and Audi, where divisional managing directors are represented on the Board of Directors.

To sum up, the results of privatisation have been:

- to consolidate and improve SEAT's standing and image;
- to improve the financial health of the company;
- to increase SEAT's share of sales in foreign markets;
- to upgrade the quality of production and goods;
- to rationalise the purchase of materials;
- to modernise factory installations;
- to increase production and productivity;
- to bring about a change in employer-employee relations.

SEAT's relationship with its investors has not changed, since the company is not on the Spanish Stock Exchange.

Supplementary information about SEAT and its situation in 1990.

By 1990 SEAT was the third member of the Volkswagen-Audi Group (VAG), as well as being the largest manufacturer and exporter of cars in Spain, employing 24 500 people. SEAT's field of activity can be illustrated – see opposite.

To establish just how important SEAT is to the VAG Group, we need only look at the figures for production, staff recruitment and business transactions as percentages of VAG figures as a whole:

Production	: 15.2%
Staff	: 10.3%
Transactions	: 10.3%

SEAT

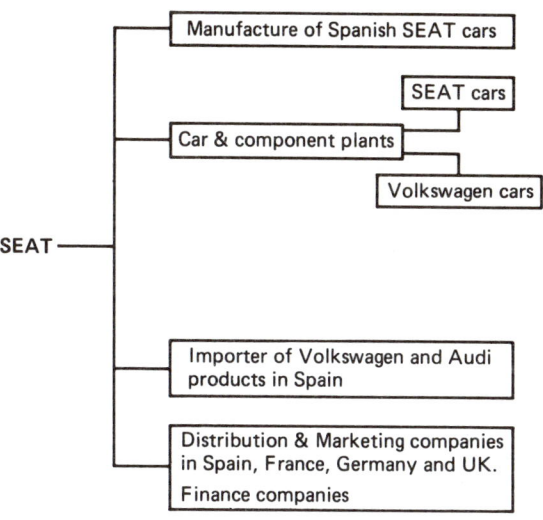

There are presently three factories in Barcelona province; one in Barcelona itself, employing 17 000, the second in Prat, employing 1500, and one more in Pamplona, employing 3000. Four models are produced in these factories:

SEAT Ibiza	: 44.2% of total production
SEAT Malaga	: 7.5% of total production
SEAT Marbella and	
Terra	: 22.5% of total production
VW Polo	: 25.7% of total production

The lessons which can be learnt from the privatisation of SEAT are many, hence the interest shown by numerous business school lecturers in analysing the process. The company itself has been happy to respond to this interest, enjoying as it does excellent relations and even links with Spain's leading business schools. The most noteworthy of these is their sponsorship of a SEAT Chair of Labour Relations Studies at IESE (The Institute of Higher Business Studies), affiliated to the University of Navarra.

From another point of view, the SEAT story is very representative of, and relevant for, other car manufacturers in today's dynamic environment of mergers and take-overs. Such alliances are now a necessary response to the globalisation of the market.

3

BAA plc

Sir Norman Payne
Chairman, BAA plc (1977–1991)

The privatisation of BAA was probably the greatest challenge which the company has faced in its 25-year history. This paper describes BAA before privatisation, how the privatisation was conducted and the advantages which have been gained since the company's new status in 1987.

BAA pre-privatisation

To see how privatisation affected BAA it is first necessary to understand what the company was like beforehand. The British Airports Authority was created by the government in 1966 to include Heathrow, Gatwick and Stansted in the south-east and Prestwick in Scotland. Edinburgh was acquired in 1971 and Glasgow and Aberdeen were bought in 1975.

Before privatisation the Authority was what is termed in the UK a nationalised industry. It had a separate legal identity and Board of Management and was financially self-sufficient. However, it was still subject to a number of strict controls as follows:

- The government appointed the Board and set salary levels for both executive and non-executive members.

- It constrained the activities of the Authority to UK airport operations and management.

- It set financial targets and annual borrowing limits and it required all long-term borrowing to be made from a central government pool. This led to conflicts between the government's financial objectives (to reduce borrowing) and those of the Authority (to complete its programme of airport developments).

Significant new competition between BAA and other airports would consequently be difficult for the government to generate. The government thus had to consider the best form of regulation for the BAA's monopolistic elements. This was done by passing legislation entitled 'The Airports Act 1986', which established BAA's regulation and its relations with its primary regulator, the Civil Aviation Authority (CAA). There are four main elements to this:

1. All BAA airports are required to apply for a permission to levy airport charges. These permissions contain additional conditions relating to the airport accounts. The latter have to show income and expenditure attributable to levying of airport charges and operational activities, as well as funding from other entities within the BAA group.

2. The CAA can at any time impose conditions on any aviation-related activities at airports where permissions are granted. The CAA can therefore impose rulings on:

- trade practices or pricing policies which are discriminatory or unfairly exploit its bargaining position;

- predatory pricing to harm other airports.

3. However, the third element comprises the main burden. Under this the BAA's three south-east airports are 'designated' for economic regulation. Airport charges are limited to a

maximum increase of the rate of inflation (RPI) minus 1 per cent for the period 1987–92 for Heathrow, Gatwick and the three south-east airports as a whole. In addition, BAA are entitled to increase airport charges to compensate for 75 per cent of any additional security costs caused by changes to Government security requirements. In detail the formula is more complex, because inflation is forecast and corrections are allowable for differences in actual charges paid per passenger.

4. The fourth element is that at the end of every five years the CAA sends a report to the UK Monopolies and Mergers Commission (MMC) reporting on how the formula could be changed for the next five years. The MMC then undertakes a review of the BAA's activities at its south-east airports and recommends what the formula should be for the next quinquennium. It also reports on BAA's operational activities and airport charges as a whole to see if any have been conducted 'against the public interest'. It can then impose conditions to remedy any such activities.

So, in general, the regulators are very powerful. They control BAA's airport charges, profitability and financial viability of new investment.

Controlling strategic resources

Having solved the problem regulating monopolistic elements, the government's second task was to consider how to control the BAA's strategic resources. In other words, how could the government stop airport assets being sold to, for instance, housing developers or airline groups?

This particular problem was solved in three ways:

- Firstly, the government holds a special 'golden' share of no value or voting power. However, certain matters require the special shareholder's prior consent.

- Secondly, BAA's Articles of Association restrict any person or group of people acting together from holding more than 15 per cent of voting rights. This rule can only be changed with the special shareholder's consent.

- Thirdly, the sale of airport assets at Heathrow, Gatwick and Stansted can only be carried out with the special shareholder's consent.

The process of privatisation

Having decided on these matters the privatisation process could begin. In August 1986 the old British Airports Authority was extinguished and its rights, obligations and assets transferred to BAA plc. At this stage all shares in the company were owned by the government. In addition, the group was restructured with BAA as the holding company serviced by a small corporate office in London. Five 100 per cent owned subsidiaries (Heathrow, Gatwick, Stansted and Scottish Airports plus British Airport Services Limited) were created. The latter was created as a company providing a range of special services to the airports.

The new BAA plc could now be floated on the London Stock Exchange. A prospectus for sale was issued in July 1987 inviting potential investors to purchase shares in the new company. The prospectus covered five years of accounting information, a review of BAA's business, the validity of BAA's title to property and assets and a listing of material factors affecting the company's future prospects. The price was fixed at £2.45 per share in line with Stock Market valuations at the time of flotations, with 500 million shares being put up for sale. The general public was offered up to 260 million at the fixed price. In addition, 115 million shares were placed at the fixed price with financial institutions. The remaining 125 million shares were subject to a tender offer, i.e. institutions and members of the public could bid for the shares with the fixed price being the minimum. Some private placement of shares was also made in Canada.

In the event, shares were oversubscribed about eight times and the government raised £1.3 billion. The number of shareholders was initially about 2 million, most of whom were only allocated a minimum of 100 shares. However, this number has since reduced to about 750,000, despite the existence of a share bonus scheme for those holding on to their shares until July 1990.

Advantages gained from privatisation

Having gone through the privatisation process, the company has enjoyed four main benefits from privatisation:

1. BAA has been able to diversify into areas closely related to the air transport industry, as follows:

- Firstly, cargo handling. BAA has entered this market with a company called Skycare which now has warehousing at or around all our major airports. Not only will this prove profitable, but it will also increase the choice of handlers available for airlines and the competitiveness of this sector of the market.

- Secondly, hotels. The hotel group now owns hotels at the three south-east airports as well as equity stakes in projects at other non-airport locations in the UK and on the continent. Again, this should not only provide a financial return, but also improve the facilities available to airport customers.

- Thirdly, in 1988 BAA bought a property company called Lynton. This was in order to improve the property potential of airport land by bringing in commercial skills and knowledge. Airline customers are already gaining from this by the construction of catering bases for SAS at Gatwick and

British Airways at Heathrow and a maintenance area for British Midland at Heathrow.

- Fourthly, BAA has just received Parliamentary Assent to build and operate a dedicated, high-speed rail link between Heathrow and the centre of London, cutting the journey time to only 16 minutes. BAA is funding 80 per cent of this £250m project. Not only will this be a commercial operation, but the overall level of service and international competitiveness of Heathrow will also be improved.

- Lastly, privatisation has enabled BAA to become more involved in international projects – in particular, at Macau and Gibraltar, as well as commercial management at Pittsburgh, USA.

2. BAA now has access to capital markets; it can borrow from commercial sources to finance development plans and there are now relationships with 30 banks. This range allows the company to use several types of finance, ranging from the European Investment Bank (probably BAA's most important single source of finance) through to short-term dollar and sterling commercial paper.

3. The third benefit is that BAA is now free to undertake truly international tendering for the procurement of its goods and services. As our aim is to maximise shareholder returns, it is critical that procurement should provide the best value for money rather than bow to Government pressures to buy national purchasing. In the past few years BAA has advertised tenders extensively in the EEC's Official Journal and has bought services and equipment from all over the world.

4. The fourth benefit is that BAA can now offer its staff a share in the business. Participation rates are very high: 70 per cent of staff own shares and 52 per cent contribute to a monthly savings scheme, enabling them to buy shares at advantageous rates. Remuneration can also be more closely tied to market rates of pay and bonuses can be paid

according to performance against agreed targets. This helps motivate staff by bringing their interests and those of the company closer together.

However, it should also be mentioned that privatisation seems to have worked in terms of BAA's performance. Profits have increased from £124m in 1987/88 to £256m in 1989/90, an annual increase of 27 per cent. Passengers have increased over the same period from 63m to 74m. The share price has increased from £2.45 in July 1987 to over £4 today and has out-performed the market overall. Perhaps more importantly, BAA's commitment to improved service standards and increased capacity has continued with capital investment planned at £1.2 billion for the next five years. Since privatisation, the £200m North Terminal at Gatwick and the £100m refurbishment of Heathrow's Terminal 3 have been completed. In March 1991 the new terminal at Stansted, costing £400m, was opened. This has an annual passenger capacity of eight million per annum with easy extension to fifteen million and land safeguarded for a second terminal. At Heathrow, work is under way to extend Terminal 4 and a new pier is being built for domestic passengers in Terminal 1. In Scotland there is a long term redevelopment programme for Glasgow, with the first phase costing £60m.

The challenges from privatisation

Having listed the benefits from privatisation, what can be said about the challenges arising from it?

First, there is the need to maintain good relations with the company's regulators. However, the terms of regulation are established in law and are much easier to manage for BAA's long-term business than pre-privatisation Government regulations.

The second problem is on a more technical note. The RPI−x+S formula is too rigid when external costs are imposed on BAA which are beyond its control, for example the loss of intra-EC duty-free income, the possible need to screen all hold baggage, or the costs of EC/Non-EC passenger segregation at airports. Under the present formula prices can only be adjusted after these events have happened, so that compensation might only be received two or three years later. This represents an enormous financing cost to BAA. However, BAA is discussing with its regulators the possibility of having 'triggers' to allow for immediate compensation which should hopefully overcome this problem.

Lastly, as well as pleasing its airline and passenger customers, BAA now has to devote resources to managing its financial partners and shareholders. However, in this respect BAA is no different from any other private sector company, although there is a particular requirement to communicate the long-term nature of the airport business compared with the more short-term horizons of our bankers and the financial institutions who own around 75 per cent of BAA shares.

Conclusion

On balance, then, BAA feels that the benefits from its privatisation far outweigh the challenges; the financial and operational track record over the 1987–91 period certainly proves this. The form of BAA's privatisation (i.e. a 100 per cent outright sale plus economic regulation) is obviously not going to be the most appropriate in all situations. However, the company feels it is a much superior form of airport privatisation than exists in the USA, for instance, where airlines own their own terminal buildings.

4

BRITISH AIRWAYS

David Burnside
Director of Public Affairs, British Airways plc

The ancient Chinese, it is said, had a special malediction for their enemies: 'May you live in interesting times.'

British Airways has probably lived in more interesting times than any other major company in Britain. In less than twenty years it has moved from disastrously unsuccessful state ownership to established success in the private sector; from bankruptcy to financial prosperity; from domestic ridicule to international distinction. As a result, its transfer to the private sector took longer, and encountered more obstacles along the road, than that of any other of the dozen or so major British enterprises that have so far been privatised.

At one time, British Airways looked as if it might be the first British industry out of the privatisation starting gate. In July 1979, shortly after the election that brought Margaret Thatcher to power, the new Secretary of State for Trade and Industry, John Nott, announced that the Government was to sell 'a substantial minority' of shares in the airline to the investing public. The meaning of a substantial minority was not spelt out, but there was a general assumption that it would be about 45 per cent. There was no indication of when the sale would take place, but again, it was assumed that it might be a couple of years or so before the airline was ripe for the market. In fact, it was to be nearly eight years before the public would be invited to buy, not a minority, but the entire share capital of the airline.

Between 1979 and 1987, as the airline wrestled with problem after problem, the most optimistic advocate of privatisation might have wondered if British Airways were ever going to enter the private sector. At times, he might have wondered if it were going to survive at all.

For a quarter of a century after the Second World War, British civil aviation was mainly in the hands of a pair of state corporations. British European Airways (BEA) was responsible for scheduled services within Europe and the UK, and British Overseas Airways Corporation (BOAC) for intercontinental routes. Privately-owned airlines, some of substantial size, were permitted to operate charter services, but were seldom allowed to expand deeply into the scheduled service field. Had they been left as separate entities, privatisation of either or both the state corporations might have been relatively quick and easy. In those days, however, privatisation was on nobody's political agenda. Successive Conservative governments were as content as Labour ones to regard state ownership as the natural order of things.

In 1972, as part of a new government civil aviation policy, the two corporations were brought together under the name of British Airways. It was not a happy marriage. The two airlines had widely differing organisations and management styles. Their workforces regarded each other with suspicion and hostility, and their managements strove to retain as much of their old autonomy as they could.

Not until 1976 did a single organisation with a common management structure emerge, and even then, British Airways was little more than a name among large sections of the workforce, who resisted efforts to bring about full integration or new working practices. The new airline commanded little loyalty among employees who clung to the traditions of their vanished companies. It was not a healthy climate in which to bring about the drastic rationalisation that might alone have justified the merger.

The 1970s were good years for the airline industry. Passenger and cargo growth of 10 per cent or more each year was normal. In the space of two years in the late 1970s, the number of passengers carried on British Airways scheduled services rose by nearly 30 per cent. Between 1972 and 1980, British Airways returned a profit before interest and tax in every single year, and an operating surplus in every year except one. Those profits were nothing like large enough, however, to meet the massive investment in new aircraft and equipment that the airline needed. On the other hand, the fact that it was earning a profit at all made it difficult to persuade the management and workforce, or even the government for that matter, that fundamental changes were becoming essential as fuel and labour costs rose remorselessly in the later 1970s.

The problems were formidable and deep-seated. Cost levels were alarmingly high. British Airways had inherited a mixed bag of over two hundred aircraft, including many small and heterogeneous fleets of obsolete 'gas guzzlers'. Finding two nominally similar aircraft with the same seating capacity or the same galley equipment was a constant headache for the people who had to run the airline from day to day.

Aircraft utilisation was low. Ground equipment was often old and unreliable. Punctuality was poor and declining. Aircraft were shabby and service indifferent. The considerable pool of public goodwill that the airline had inherited from its predecessors was steadily evaporating as customers drew unflattering comparisons with foreign and domestic competitors. Not suprisingly, staff morale was in shreds.

Costs were high largely because the airline was grossly overmanned. The economies of scale that might have been the principal benefit of the merger had never been realised. As managers struggled to cope with mushrooming business and inadequate resources, staff numbers were allowed to drift upwards, year after year, until by the summer of 1979, they peaked at over fifty-eight thousand. In the mid-1970s, staff productivity was never better than 60 per cent of that of international competitors. A leading American analyst calculated that British Airways had about twice as many managerial and administrative staff as most of its competitors. Senior managers would admit privately that the airline had at least ten thousand too many staff.

The airline's board had indeed a plan for raising productivity and lowering costs dramatically. It was based, not on reducing staff numbers, but on doubling the number of passengers carried over eight years while holding staff numbers steady. To carry the extra passengers, the airline would invest nearly two and a half billion pounds in new and more efficient aircraft. That in itself would call for a massive increase in borrowings and therefore in interest charges.

It would have been a bold plan at the best of times. But the end of the 1970s was no longer the best of times. Competition was increasing, and economic storm clouds were gathering on the world's horizons. In the summer of 1980, the storm broke. The long boom in business collapsed. Passenger numbers, instead of rising as the plan required, fell by over 5 per cent. Seat occupancy rates slumped. Ironically, just as the long-awaited new aircraft were finally being delivered at great expense, one and a half million British Airways passengers disappeared almost overnight. Airlines all over the world, struggling to fill empty seats, joined in a price war that sent fares tumbling and losses soaring.

Despite urgent short-term cost-cutting measures, British Airways found itself at the end of its financial year with a loss of £141 million, by far the worst result it had ever returned. Revenue results were bad, and the cost of new aircraft was plunging the airline deeply into debt.

At the beginning of 1981, at the height of the economic gale, a leading British industrialist, Sir John King, took over as the airline's new chairman. A dedicated believer in private enterprise, his brief had been to prepare the state-owned airline for public sale. In the event, his first priority was to save it from financial collapse.

In September 1981, with recession still raging and losses running at two hundred pounds a minute, Sir John announced the most dramatic retrenchment programme any major British enterprise had undergone for half a century. Nine thousand jobs were to go in nine months, cutting the wage bill by two million pounds a week. Routes were to be withdrawn, stations and engineering bases closed, aircraft, offices and subsidiary companies sold off. Nothing less could ensure survival in what the airline described bluntly as the worst crisis in its history.

Tough and unpalatable as they undoubtedly were, Sir John's measures saved the day. True, the cost of cutting staff and writing down assets, added to interest charges on new aircraft, pushed the 1981–82 deficit to an astronomical £545 million, so that the airline was technically bankrupt. But most of this was in 'once-for-all' extraordinary charges designed to free the airline from the financial burden of past policies. The drastic surgery transformed the situation. Within a year costs had fallen, load factors were up sharply, and staff productivity had risen dramatically. Freed from the massive burden of surplus staff and obsolete aircraft, the airline was once again trading profitably. Nine years later, it still is.

With costs under control, a healthy balance sheet, and a rising level of profitability, the first major hurdle to privatisation had been cleared. Perhaps for the first time since British Airways had been formed, it was possible to envisage a day when the airline would be a sound long-term investment. As profitability rose and cash flow improved, British Airways began to invest large sums in new aircraft, ground equipment, computer systems, cabin equipment, and all the other items that had been starved of cash for years.

Civil aviation, however, is a service industry. Modern aircraft and equipment count for little unless the passenger sees the airline not simply as technically efficient but as a caring human organisation dedicated to making his or her journey as trouble-free and enjoyable as possible. The creation of such a reputation would be essential to a successful transfer to the private sector.

Early in 1983 a new chief executive, Colin Marshall, had joined the airline after an outstandingly successful career in the vehicle rental business in Europe and the USA. One of his most important tasks would be to transform the company's image and public reputation. A striking new corporate livery was adopted for all aircraft, ground equipment, ticket offices and other premises world-wide. As part of the same process, some twenty-eight thousand staff world-wide were kitted out in completely new uniforms. Both moves were intended to convey, to customers and staff alike, a complete break with the past.

The most important ingredient of success, however, would be the attitude of staff towards their customers. Unless they were perceived as friendly, understanding and genuinely helpful, then a glossy new corporate image would only emphasise the gulf between the implied promise and the actual performance. For enduring success, the airline must be run at every level by people who really wanted to do a good job for their customers, and who believed that their management was trying to help them to do it.

To bring about this transformation in the human face of the airline, British Airways began one of the longest and most successful in-house staff training programmes ever devised. The initial programme, known as 'Putting People First', involved thirty-five thousand staff around the world and stressed the importance of personal attitudes, not only towards the customer, but towards colleagues and neighbours. It was the progenitor of a series of courses which were to have a major influence in building staff morale and in winning for the airline a rising reputation among its customers.

While Lord King and Sir Colin Marshall, as they were to become, were revitalising the airline, the Conservative government was still intent on privatisation. On 1 April 1984, the airline duly became a public limited company called British Airways plc, albeit one in which all the shares were held for the time being by the secretary of state.

At the same time, the management was turning its attention to preparing the ground among its own workforce. Today, when a dozen major British state enterprises have successfully entered the private sector, privatisation is widely understood by the public. It is easy to forget that as recently as 1984, it was a complete mystery to most of the people who worked for those businesses. The airline's turnround had been achieved with the active support and co-operation of both workforce and unions. Even the shedding of close to 40 per cent of the workforce had provoked little resistance. It could not be said that the unions necessarily supported privatisation in the same way, but allowing for some ritual drum-beating by small militant groups, there was little organised opposition.

Research disclosed, however, a great deal of ignorance and unease among the staff about the implications. Many admitted to being in two minds: they saw the development as being good for the airline, but feared the personal consequences for themselves and their families. Specifically, there were deep-rooted fears that job security would be further threatened and that conditions of employment would deteriorate. There was also a great deal of misunderstanding about the role and influence of shareholders.

Sir Colin Marshall tackled the problem in characteristic fashion. Typical staff from throughout the organisation were invited to put their questions and views to him in an open forum that was filmed and shown at staff meetings throughout the airline. Questions that could not be answered immediately and with authority by the departmental manager were passed to the airline's internal privatisation team to be dealt with as fully and honestly as possible within the limited knowledge of the government's plans available at that time. Each question (and there were many hundreds of them) then received a personal written answer. Not all could be answered fully at that stage, but the exercise went a long way to demonstrating to staff that there were no sinister undertones to privatisation, and that the airline's management was doing all it could to keep them fully and honestly informed.

As it turned out, the privatisation of British Airways was to be so long delayed that several other leading British companies took its place in the queue. By the time the airline's turn came, most of its staff proved to be tolerably familiar with the share sale process.

By the mid-1980s, British Airways seemed to be ready for privatisation. The airline was operating profitably and expected to remain so. The debt-equity ratio was a respectable one. The aircraft fleet had been substantially modernised, and the airline's staff were offering an increasingly competitive standard of service. The outlook seemed brighter than it had ever been. But in fact, a succession of frustrations lay ahead.

In December 1983, with privatisation in mind, the Government asked the Civil Aviation Authority to review the implications for competition and for the British airline industry of privatising British Airways. In its report, the CAA called for the transfer to other British airlines of some thirty British Airways routes from Gatwick, Manchester, Aberdeen, Belfast, Birmingham, Edinburgh and Glasgow, as well as for the transfer to British Caledonian Airways of British Airways routes to Saudi Arabia.

The recommendations, which if adopted would have had serious implications for the jobs of many of the airline's employees, produced a storm within the airline. Board, management, unions and employees found themselves united as never before, perhaps, in their determination to resist the proposals. The board, led by Lord King, pointed out that the substitution of other airlines for British Airways might help those airlines, but would do nothing whatever to benefit the customer by widening competition. The workforce and unions viewed the proposals as a shoddy recompense for the years of sacrifice that they had willingly accepted in order to help the company's recovery.

The lobbying campaign that followed was possibly the most extensive, and the most successful, that had ever been undertaken by a British enterprise. Over twenty-five thousand employees signed a petition handed in at No. 10 Downing Street. Members of Parliament with airports in their constituencies were bombarded with angry letters. Many thousands of staff, from aircraft captains to office workers, collected signatures, lobbied MPs, distributed badges, T-shirts and car stickers, or explained to customers why they would be worse off if the proposals were adopted. At every level, both at home and overseas, the organisation closed ranks as it had never done before, burying in the process any lingering traces of the old company loyalties and attitudes that might have survived the dramatic events of the past five years.

From the airline's point of view, the outcome was almost completely satisfactory. A government White Paper concluded that the CAA proposals would be 'excessively disruptive' to British Airways and called instead for a relatively modest exchange of routes with British Caledonian. None the less, over a year elapsed before the competition debate was satisfactorily resolved. While it was in progress, there was no question of British Airways going to the market, if only because of the difficulty of valuing an airline whose future route structure was in doubt.

By early 1985, with the competition issue settled, there were again hopes that flotation might be on the way. Again, they were to be dashed.

In 1982, the liquidation of Laker Airways had been followed by an action alleging that a number of airlines, including British Airways, had conspired to put Laker Airways out of business. Not until October 1985 was the case settled on agreed terms, without admission of liability by the defendants. A consolidated anti-trust class action on behalf of transatlantic air passengers against a number of airlines was also settled without admission of liability early in 1986.

The settlement of these long-drawn-out legal matters might have given renewed hope of a swift transition to the private sector. But yet another problem arose.

The Anglo-US Air Services Agreement governing the operation of flights between the two countries was coming up for renewal, and serious differences arose between the two governments. The disagreement was wholly outside the control of British Airways, but the commercial consequences to the airline of a failure to agree would have been so serious that the then Minister of Transport, Nicholas Ridley, had to announce in March 1986 that, once again, the Government was unable to set a date for privatisation. In the event, the diplomatic difficulties were successfully resolved, but two further formidable obstacles rose in the path to the private sector.

That spring, the Chernobyl nuclear disaster in the USSR, in itself a major disincentive to transatlantic tourism, was accompanied by a serious outbreak of international terrorism. The two events between them brought about a catastrophic fall in bookings to Europe. Although the setback affected the entire European travel industry, it was not calculated to encourage a bullish short-term view of the airline business.

Ironically, perhaps, the vigour and imagination with which British Airways led the industry in fighting back against the unexpected recession turned out to its eventual advantage. It was seen by many as clear evidence that, after nearly a decade of vicissitudes, the airline had developed the strength and maturity of management to take the inevitable hazards of international business in its stride. By that time, perhaps, only a professional optimist could have brought himself to believe that there were no further pitfalls ahead. But in fact the end of the obstacle course had been reached.

In September 1986 the then Secretary of State for Transport, John Moore, finally made the long-delayed announcement that the share sale would take place early the following year. On 27 January 1987, the airline's prospectus announced the offer of just over 720 million 25p Ordinary shares at £1.25 per share, putting a value on the company of some £900 million.

A nation-wide publicity campaign, under the title of Britain's Highest Flying Company, was launched to support the share issue. It further reinforced the high profile that the airline already enjoyed, if enjoyed was the term, at home and abroad. For years past, British Airways had seldom been out of the headlines. The turnround from bankruptcy to consistent profitability had turned Lord King and Sir Colin Marshall into household names among millions of potential investors who would have had difficulty identifying the chairman or chief executive of any other company in Britain.

Not all financial commentators shared the view that the issue was likely to appeal to the small investor. British Airways, it was suggested in a few quarters, might prove a little too exciting for the shareholder in search of a safe, uncontentious utility. They were proved resoundingly wrong. Small investors flocked to invest in what many clearly saw as an exciting and fast-moving business. By the time the lists closed, over one million applicants had sought nearly eight billion shares, making the offer eleven times over-subscribed. Applications had to be heavily scaled down, but at the end of the day, over one million private investors received an allocation. Among the new owners of British Airways were about 97 per cent of the airline's workforce.

Today, although the British Airways shareholder register has fallen, as have those of most privatised companies, the airline still has about three hundred thousand shareholders, most of them small private investors. Moreover, the majority of the workforce continue to be shareholders in the company.

What have the airline and its shareholders gained from its transfer to the private sector? In some respects, not a great deal has changed. Civil aviation remains to a large extent a regulated industry. British Airways must still seek licences to fly international and domestic services, it must operate within the terms set by international air service agreements, and it must seek permission from the Civil Aviation Authority to raise or lower its fares. These are constraints common to the whole industry, and privatisation has made them neither more nor less onerous.

The main benefits of privatisation have been numerous. The airline is now free to make its own investment decisions, particularly on new aircraft, as it thinks fit. As a state corporation, British Airways could not buy a single aircraft, or even lease one for more than a year, without government approval. The intention was good (government intentions always are) but the results could be disastrous. Back in the 1970s, a vital re-equipment order was held up for twelve months while Whitehall sought ways to avoid a politically unpopular decision. The Treasury agonised over the financial implications, and all kinds of interested parties lobbied for an outcome that would suit their own ends. All perfectly legal and proper; that is how political decisions are reached. But meanwhile, the airline's future was hamstrung by the failure to reach what should never have been a political decision in the first place.

The board is also free to grasp business opportunities as they arise, rather than waiting on the deliberations of Whitehall. The decision to purchase British Caledonian Airways in 1987 was a classic example. Had the board not acted swiftly, that quite unexpected opportunity might never have recurred. We may imagine what would have happened if British Airways, as a state corporation, had sought to buy a major privately-owned competititor. Even if the purchase had been permitted at all, the decision would probably have been delayed for months while mandarins mused and Parliament pondered. By which time BCal might well have been out of business.

The greatest benefit, perhaps, has been the company's ability to raise money where, when and how it sees fit without being constrained by Whitehall policy. As a state corporation, British Airways was not only limited in the amount of money it was permitted to raise, regardless of need or opportunity; it was also obliged to raise it, not in the ways that best suited the airline, but those which best suited Treasury policies. Today, we can raise money as best suits us. We can make a rights issue, as we have recently done, to finance major industry investments. To acquire new aircraft, we have pioneered the operating lease, a type of finance that suits us, our bankers and our suppliers. A few years ago, we should have had to try to persuade the Treasury to approve it. We might well not have succeeded.

In anticipation of privatisation, British Airways brought in an employee profit-sharing scheme that gave staff, whether shareholders or not, a direct interest in the profitability of the company and therefore in its commercial success. Again, it is hard to believe that we should have been allowed to introduce any such incentive if we had stayed in the public sector. The evidence is that we would not.

The temptations to use (or misuse) a state airline as an instrument of public policy are very numerous, and successive British governments, at one time or another, succumbed to most of them. British Airways and its predecessors were regarded at one time or another as instruments of foreign policy, as a source of foreign exchange, and as a shop window for British industry. These are only a few examples of the things they were expected to be, not in their own interest, but in what was supposed to be that of the nation.

Today, we are free to get on with our true role as an international transport and communication business. It is a role we are good at, and at which we have been increasingly successful for nearly a decade. We are confident that we shall continue to be. As the Chinese sage might have put it, we have certainly lived in interesting times. But looking back on what we have achieved, perhaps that wasn't such a bad thing after all.

5

VICKERS SHIPBUILDING AND ENGINEERING LIMITED

Sue Kernaghan

The privatisation of Vickers Shipbuilding and Engineering had all the marks of a politically explosive situation. As a major employer and a strategically important defence contractor, VSEL was the largest and most complex of Britain's shipyard sell-offs. Everyone from the government to the City, management, and local residents had an interest in the outcome of the sale. These interests came together when an employee consortium won the bid for VSEL in 1986 — and, coincidentally, made a profit for them all.

VSEL has long played a leading role in British shipbuilding, employing 70 per cent of the industry nationally and operating, at Barrow-in-Furness, the largest single-site engineering complex in Britain. Despite its role as a virtual national resource, VSEL's public ownership was short lived. It became the defence arm of the publicly-owned British Shipbuilders in 1977 as part of the Labour Government's policy to nationalise all shipbuilding operations. The Conservative victory two years later brought in 'an overriding philosophy to denationalise everything that could be denationalised,' according to former VSEL personnel director, Rick Emslie.

The firm is best known for producing submarines, including those currently being built to carry Trident nuclear warheads, and it was these defence connections that pushed it towards privatisation. Says Emslie, 'Only the warship builders could be denationalised as they were the only shipyards with any prospect of turning a profit.' Smaller defence contractors were sold to private interests in the early 'eighties but VSEL's size, complexity and £100 million price tag kept it off the market until 1984.

Management had been interested in organising a buy-out from the first possibility of a sale. When plans to privatise were announced in 1984, the then managing director, Gregg Mott, made unfruitful enquiries to merchant banks. His successor's queries were also received unenthusiastically. 'VSEL was the biggest shipyard privatisation yet and it was strategically important; the City lacked confidence in a management buy-out of such proportions,' says Emslie.

The board opted to make the bid via an employee consortium as, explains Emslie, 'Board members knew they would need employee backing, both to raise the necessary capital and to gain government's acceptance of the bid. Though we called it an employee buy-out, it was in reality more of an institutional buy-out,' he says. 'Institutions took 73 per cent of the equity, employees 27 per cent, so perhaps "employee buy-out" was a bit of a misnomer.'

In late 1985, the new managing director, Dr Rodney Leach, made a third foray, this time to both the government and the City, to gain support for the bid. Meanwhile, the acquisitive conglomerate Trafalgar House had also expressed interest. With competitive pressure and a February 1986 bid deadline, the consortium had only two weeks to raise £75 million. Leach and other board members made a hurried round of twenty-five City institutions and succeeded in raising the necessary funds.

It was a hectic time for the board. 'During the buy-out, four directors spent all their time on the buy-out, while the balance looked after the shop. It was all very much a team effort,' says Emslie. They succeeded. In February 1986 the government declared the consortium to be the preferred bidder. 'Some say Trafalgar House's bid was the same, some say bigger, but it was hard to compare as part of the consortium's payment was deferred,' says Emslie. 'In the end I believe the government leaned towards the consortium as it is in favour of employee share-ownership.'

Local reactions to privatisation were mixed in the early days. Says Emslie: 'The people of Barrow and Birkenhead, despite having a Conservative MP, are basically labour supporters. They didn't particularly favour privatisation, but when it appeared to be inevitable they preferred an employee buy-out.'

A survey sponsored by the consortium in late November and early December of 1985 found that 91 per cent of the Barrow adult population were aware of the intention to privatise the shipyard and 73 per cent of these knew of the consortium bid. Among employees, opinion tended to favour privatisation but not strongly, with 56 per cent in favour, 15 per cent against and the remainder neutral or undecided. Of those against the sale, 43 per cent cited concern about redundancies and unemployment as reasons for their misgivings. Significantly, half the sample thought no one would oppose the consortium bid.

When asked how likely they would be to buy shares if loans were made available on easy terms, 35 per cent of employees said they would definitely or probably buy. As it happened, an astonishing 82 per cent of VSEL's fifteen thousand employees bought shares. 'We based our initial projections on National Freight's experience,' says Emslie. 'Forty per cent of its employees bought shares and we aimed for that as a benchmark. But the idea really gained momentum and, in the end, the response was overwhelming.'

Because of VSEL's close ties with the local community, management also offered shares to Barrow and Birkenhead residents, five thousand of whom invested. By numbers alone, 90 per cent of initial shareholders lived in Barrow or Birkenhead either as employees, VSEL pensioners or local residents.

The yard's strategic importance was not forgotten either. The government still holds what is known as a 'golden share' — a single non-voting share allowing it to veto matters of policy relating to ownership. Further, no single shareholder can hold more than 15 per cent of VSEL shares.

'At first employees and local people were sceptical about share ownership and we had to sell the whole concept. Key members of VSEL's fourteen trade unions were interested, and that helped us gain support for the idea,' says Emslie. There were certainly plenty of incentives to buy. 'We were the first company to subsidise interest-free loans for employee share purchases, and the first to arrange with the City for additional free shares. The consortium offered 150 free shares to employees buying 500, so, because they were getting 650 shares for the price of 500, the effective price of the £1 shares was only 77p.' Employees could thus make a profit on the day the shares began trading and many did take that route, with a large sell-off by employees at a price of £1.55. Many more sold when, strengthened by a renewed Conservative victory in 1987, the share price quickly moved to a peak of £6.50. In 1990, over 2500 employees still held shares, down from an initial peak of over 11 000.

Employee ownership is, in theory, expected to provide incentives for greater staff productivity and loyalty. In fact, a large proportion of employees thought that would be the case; the pre-bid survey found 36 per cent of staff and residents believed ownership would provide an incentive for employees to work harder. 'Productivity has improved,' says Emslie, 'but with so many variables changing at the same time, it's hard to judge the precise impact of privatisation.'

Nor does he believe that employee ownership has had a major impact on loyalty to the firm. Barrow is a special situation, he explains. 'The community has always been very much tied up with the shipyards. In Barrow, VSEL employs thirteen thousand people — almost a third of the working population. Generations of the same family have worked here and had strong feelings about the yard, so employee ownership hasn't had as much of an impact as it might have elsewhere.'

This point was brought home in 1988, when share ownership did not prevent employees from striking against the firm they technically owned. 'Shortly after the privatisation, we brought about some changes in working practices. There were no redundancies involved but we wanted to get rid of flexible holidays and break down some of the traditional demarcations. Because a lot of work was coming through there was an element of disbelief among the workforce that things had to change,' says Emslie. 'Share ownership did not affect the workforce's thinking in negotiations, nor did we really expect it to. Employees are understandably more concerned with their weekly wage packets than with long-term share prices.' Ironically, the share price remained buoyant throughout the short strike and took a dip the moment it ended.

'The strike was ostensibly about the issue of flexible holidays, but the underlying issue was one of acceptance of change in the new commercial circumstances,' says Emslie. These new commercial circumstances had as much to do with changes in Ministry of Defence policy as they did with privatisation.

The MoD was and remains far and away Vickers's largest customer, accounting for 98 per cent of the order book. In the mid-1980s the ministry stopped the traditional cost-plus contracts and demanded tighter delivery deadlines. As a result, VSEL management were forced to adopt a more commercial orientation. A history of government contracts and technically complex products had made it easy, even inevitable, that VSEL should have become product driven. 'The MoD forced us to become more cost driven, but making management aware of this was difficult, and is not yet wholly complete,' says Emslie.

Privatisation has certainly helped change management attitudes. 'Now that the company is managed in Barrow and is no longer a subsidiary of British Shipbuilders, we have been able to cut out a lot of bureaucracy and layers of communication,' says Emslie. 'Top management were thrilled to have the freedom to make decisions without referring to head office, especially as that freedom made it a lot easier to implement changes. Middle management, however, found it harder to get used to, as they had not been in the thick of the buy-out.'

Of course, having investors to answer to has also changed management orientations. 'We suddenly had another player to inform and had to get used to communicating with them,' says Emslie.

VSEL has also modernised its production processes through a £200 million investment programme. This was started just before privatisation and the consortium took over the responsibility of paying the final £90 million of the commitment. 'Unfortunately, the productivity per employee is still below the leaders in the engineering sector,' says Emslie. As Rodney Leach told *The Financial Times* in 1987: 'It would be wrong to say privatisation suddenly transformed things, but it gave more credibility to management, and a climate of better understanding has developed.'

Employee ownership also helped remove some of the secrecy relating to management policy in the warship-building industry. 'Better communications helped us to construct milestones. People no longer do their jobs not knowing how they fit into the whole picture.' said Leach.

For the future, that picture may include a reduced dependency on the MoD. Emslie admits that the recent outbreak of peace could dampen the defence market. But he thinks that should not hurt the demand for submarines too much, as they play more of a defence role than the more offence-oriented land forces. 'VSEL still has a monopoly in submarines in the UK, but that doesn't prevent the government from driving a much harder bargain. It is still a monopoly buyer, after all,' says Emslie. 'Realistically there is a need to get into fields other than defence, and to reduce the dependence on the MoD. Our strategy had two planks: to spread the customer base in defence through exports, and to diversify into non-defence markets.'

Exporting so far has been less than successful: VSEL has had no major overseas orders before or after privatisation, although a sale of nuclear-powered submarines to the Canadian government was near completion before a last-minute cancellation. 'Exporting warships is highly political and very long term, as marketing is done on a government to government basis,' says Emslie.

'VSEL's current output on the non-defence side will take a while with existing facilities, but with an acquisition programme the process can be speeded up,' he says.

Overall, Emslie believes that VSEL has benefited from the change to private ownership: 'VSEL is more profitable now but not yet profitable enough. The time-scale of the company's products is so long that the impact of change takes a long time to filter through. Many of the changes in management thinking would have occurred anyway because of changing MoD demands. But either way, there has been a renaissance — one could say that privatisation brought together all the strands.'

6

COMPAGNIE FINANCIÈRE DE SUEZ

Compagnie Financière de Suez (CFS) was one of France's largest privatisations. As France's leading financial group in terms of income and fifty-eighth in the world in terms of assets, the 130-year-old company was an attractive asset for any investment portfolio.

Background to the company

CFS had a long history as a private company before it was nationalised. It was set up in 1858 by Ferdinand de Lesseps to dig and operate the Suez canal linking the Red Sea to the Mediterranean. When the Suez canal was nationalised by the Egyptian government in 1956, the company, then called Compagnie Universelle du Canal Maritime de Suez, had to change its emphasis. In 1958 it changed its name to Compagnie Financière de Suez and established a banking arm in the following year. By 1966, the Banque de la Compagnie de Suez had merged with the banking activities of Union de Mines-La Henin. It also acquired its first industrial interest in Pont-à-Mousson. The growth continued in 1969, when Suez prepared to merge Saint Gobain with Pont-à-Mousson. Other notable mergers included the takeover of Banque de L'Indochine which gave the enlarged company a substantial international base.

The company came under state ownership in the round of nationalisations instigated by the Socialist government in the late 'seventies and early 'eighties. However, during its brief time as a nationalised enterprise, the company retained many of the characteristics of a private sector operation. In 1985, three years after the initial nationalisation, Banque La Henin and Banque Sofinco, Banque Vernes et Commerciale de Paris and Banque Parisienne de Crédit joined the group. In the mid-1980s, it was still showing an interest in major international projects, such as the launch of Eurotunnel and the Eurodisneyland project.

On the eve of the flotation

By 1987, it had offices in eighty-five countries. The company now comprised the banking network of the Banque Indosuez group which covered sixty-five countries, Suez International, venture capital businesses such as the Suez Technology Fund in the USA, and Suez Asia development capital in South-East Asia. It had also teamed up with the Matuschka Group in Germany and with Thompson Clive in Britain.

It ranked high among the premier French and European financial groups both in net worth and consolidated earnings. CFS was now a broadly diversified financial group with compatible interests in banking and insurance, manufacturing and services, and a portfolio of real estate and investment securities. The group also had a defined strategy: to develop and capitalise on its three major activities of insurance and banking, real estate, and manufacturing services. It had twenty thousand employees, most of whom were employed by Banque Indosuez and its subsidiaries.

The holding company, Suez, acted as goal-setter for the group rather than as a day-to-day manager. It preserved the autonomy, management flexibility and profit responsibility of the various operating companies. Since it has always been historically oriented to markets outside France, the Suez group held an important position in international banking through its operating arm Banque Indosuez, as well as in the international services, transportation and trade. In the four years before the sell-off, net income had grown almost three times and return on equity had risen from under 10 per cent to 14.4 per cent between 1982 and 1986.

Carefully orchestrated to interest as many potential share-holders as possible, the Suez flotation followed the media fanfare approach of British privatisations. Fearing that the French were indifferent to the privatisation, it used Catherine Deneuve, the seductive film star, in advertisements on television, the radio and in the press. The result was that shares were oversubscribed, although the price was affected by the stock market crash of 1987.

Prior to the sell-off, the company was predicting continued although more moderate growth, with capital gains levelling off following several years of very strong growth. In the favourable market conditions of the late 'eighties, these estimates proved to be underestimates of future performance.

Post privatisation

Because it had such a long history in the private sector and was only nationalised for a relatively short space of time, the company did not have the same problems readjusting to life as a private company. It had not developed bureaucratic systems and structure, nor had it radically changed its policies or strategy. Once privatised, it continued to pursue a policy of obtaining a controlling stake in the few companies that were leaders in their fields. For example, in 1988 it acquired a majority interest in Société Générale de Belgique, a leader in non-ferrous metals, cement, electricity, utilities and maritime activities, and a controlling stake in the Victoire-Colonia insurance group in 1989. As a result of such acquisitions, the

Suez group employs over a hundred thousand people world-wide.

Earnings per share rose from FF34.63 in 1987 to FF40.13 in 1989. In 1988 gross assets were estimated at FF45 billion,and by 1989 this had risen to FF73 billion. In that time, market capitalization had risen from FF33 billion to FF53 billion.

Traditionally strongest in the banking sector, Suez has now, thanks to recent acquisitions, achieved balance among its interests in banking, insurance, industry and real estate. By 1989, its total assets had grown from FF20 billion to reach FF70 billion. Its market capitalization by the end of 1989 was one of the five largest on the Paris bourse, and was spread among nearly one million stockholders. By 1989 the shareholder structure was composed of 40 per cent shareholders represented on the board, 37 per cent the general public, 20 per cent other large shareholders, and 3 per cent employee shareholding.

7

WESSEX WATER

Deborah Snow

'This is £21.8 million down the plughole. I find the water commercials quite outrageous — they seem to be gratuitously telling us that we never had water until people thought about privatising it.' *Anthony Beaumont-Dark MP, on the amount of money being spent on advertising water privatisation in 'The Times', 26 August 1989*

'The idea of spending that much money telling people that water comes from the clouds, runs downhill and goes through pipes is complete fatuous.' *Andrew Lees, Friends of the Earth, 28 August 1989*

Wessex is one of the smaller water authorities but since privatisation it has already gained a name for itself as a forward-thinking company, willing to use modern management techniques and with a coherent public relations policy.

History of the organisation while in the public sector

Until 1973, local authorities and statutory water companies provided water to the population of Britain, while local authorities were mostly responsible for sewerage treatment. The water industry was substantially reorganised in 1973 with the implementation of the 1973 Water Act. This set up ten regional authorities based on river basin catchment areas. These were responsible for water supply and sewerage services resource planning, pollution control, fisheries, land drainage, flood protection, water recreation and conservation. Under the Act, local authorities appointed the majority of Water Authority board members. The chairman and other members were appointed by the government. By 1983, the board had been reduced to 15 members, appointed by the government.

In September 1989, these water authorities were turned into private companies. Certain of their activities, such as pollution control, water resource management, flood protection, and land drainage, plus certain rights and liabilities, could not be carried out by profit-making enterprises so these were transferred to the National Rivers Authority, a new public body. In order to improve the quality of the water and carry out necessary renovation work, the government allocated each water company a 'k' factor, the amount above the retail price index by which it could increase its charges. Under this system, Wessex had to charge 4.5 per cent above the index for ten years to raise the capital necessary. This was worked out after assessing the state of the works, estimating how much the authority would have to spend to comply with future legislation, predicted population growth, and capital and operating costs.

Preparing for privatisation

Wessex is in the prosperous south-west of England and has one of the fastest residential growth rates in the country. According to the Water Share Offers Prospectus, the resident population is estimated to be increasing at a rate above the national average. Between 1985 and 1989, the population grew by 3 per cent and, based upon county planning forecasts, it will grow by another 7 per cent by 2001. Wessex provides water supplies to over 475 000 premises and disposes of sewerage from about one million domestic, industrial and commercial premises mainly in Avon, Dorset, Somerset, and Wiltshire. It shares the region with four local statutory water companies who supply 56 per cent of the water.

Even before the float, Wessex had stolen a march on the other nine water companies by winning a prestigious award in the run-up to the flotation. A complex handicapping system had been put in place by the government to ensure that none of the authorities had any advantages at the sell-off. Chairmen and senior executives were given instructions not to give interviews that would entail 'selling' their company more than any other. But Wessex, which always prided itself on its use of high technology, particularly in dealing with customer queries and problems, was highly commended in 1989 in the annual awards of the British Quality Association. The organisation, which had been rationalising and investing in modern technology for about nine years prior to privatisation, was among one of the first service organisations to receive the top award.

In the months before the sell-off, Wessex avoided some of the controversy. For example, writs were issued against eight of the ten former water authorities in November 1989 by fifteen local authorities seeking compensation for the sale of what they claimed were their assets. At stake was over £13 billion of assets transferred from local authority control in 1974 when the water authorities were set up. Only Northumbrian and Wessex were not involved in this legal wrangle.

The companies prepared a thick prospectus outlining in detail each business and its activities in order to help prospective shareholders decide in which company to buy shares. According to John Coppack, regulation and investment accountant at Wessex Water, this meant that Wessex was forced to identify what its core business was: 'This helped clear up a number of misconceptions abour our customer base. We had to make statements describing the business and the extent to which we relied on our core business of processing water. We found that we weren't able to prove that we did things we had always believed we did. It also highlighted our strengths, such as sophisticated equipment and consultancy capabilities.'

In the sell-off, the high-profile Thames Water was billed as the best buy, partly because of its location in one of the most prosperous parts of the country, but also because its management was aiming at an aggressive diversification strategy. This aimed to earn half the profits from non-core businesses within five years. Even before the float, Thames had bought a well-known international water business. Anglian was popular because of its high growth potential in the fastest growing region in Britain and because of its modern installations. Anglian was, however, handicapped by low rainfall and intensive cereal farming, which has generated an unacceptable level of nitrates in the soil. Yorkshire was also popular because its chairman was the leader in the privatisation negotiations and it looked like a soundly managed business.

Some of the worst buys were seen as South West and North West. The former served a part of the country hit by drought and pollution, and North West had a backlog of problems left over from the industrial revolution, including a heavily polluted River Mersey and crumbling sewers in the major cities in its area. Wessex Water had none of these problems and few of the advantages, so it was perceived as a fair buy along with companies such as Trent and Southern.

The ten boards splashed out over £20 million advertising, and the government spent a similar amount on its own campaign. Customers country-wide were bombarded with information via a television campaign, posters and even letters sent to private homes. This extravaganza did lead to a substantial amount of public criticism. According to Colin Chapman in *Selling the Family Silver*, the Independent Broadcasting Authority lodged 113 complaints about the use of taxpayers' money.

To encourage a wider share ownership, water company customers received a discount on shares of the company in their area. They could also invest in as many of the other companies as they could afford to, though without a discount.

Because parts of the Wessex area are supplied with water by statutory water companies, people in these areas were still eligible for discounted Wessex shares since their sewage was processed by the company. In the event, the flotation was vastly oversubscribed and the proportion of people who took their profits immediately was relatively small. In part, this was because the water sell-off encouraged people to hang on to their shares with a bonus scheme. If the small investor held on to his or her shares for more than a specified amount of time, then they would be eligible for a certain number of free shares.

Structural changes in the run-up to the sell-off

The organisation had to create a new structure and set up a legal framework in the twelve months leading up to the change-over. The company restructured in October 1988. Two water and sewerage divisions were based in Poole and Bath, supported by centralised service departments and using an integrated communications network. In preparation for the formation of the National Rivers Authority, a Wessex Rivers Unit was established at Bridgwater. This would take over all the activities which were to be transferred to the NRA in 1989.

Wessex Water plc holds the licence to process water. Wessex Water Operational Services Ltd and Wessex Business Services Ltd are the principal companies within the group which carry this out. The company also had to set up a finance department to deal with all the businesses. Wessex Water Commercial Ltd provides services that the old water authority did not provide, such as plumbing and insurance services and consultancy services. Coppack explains: 'Before privatisation we often offered our services abroad as consultants. We used to go to Africa and advise on billing software because we had developed sophisticated systems for our own operations. Since such consultancy was not a major part of the licensed business, we decided to include this operation under the commercial services operation. Wessex has now entered into a joint venture to do this with Wimpey. Wimpey Wessex Water now acts as an engineering consultant, principally abroad.' In addition, Wessex Water has sophisticated screening equipment to analyse water samples. It now offers this screening service to local health authorities for cervical smears.

Staff relations

Up to privatisation, the company was shedding staff. In 1985 the company employed 2014 people; by 1989 this had fallen to 1844. 'It is fair to say that, since privatisation, the trend in employment figures for the original water business has continued downwards, but thanks to our other operating companies we can report a slight overall increase,' reports Coppack.

In November 1989, Wessex withdrew from national pay negotiating machinery and it now negotiates with its staff as a separate unit. It has also introduced performance related pay and allocated specific objectives to specific employees.

Changes in management style

The concept of quality as an issue had started in America and had already been implemented in many of Britain's leading companies. About twelve months before privatisation, Wessex adopted a 'Quality First' approach. At the same time, it asked designers to fashion a corporate logo.

To supplement the quality programme, the company organised Wessex '90 and Wessex '91, events which highlight the importance of total quality in all systems and procedures. Each day-long event brings together all staff and serves as a forum for developing the new company's culture. For Wessex '90, the company hired a showground just outside Bristol for a day of presentations and discussions. Coppack says: 'It was an opportunity for staff to get to know our new identity, meet senior managers and enjoy a constructive day's discussion.' Previously such an event would have been unheard of.

Customer relations

Customers now come much higher on the agenda at Wessex. At board level there is now a director of customer services and information systems. Customer services has been split between Bristol and Poole. Coppack explains: 'We upped the profile of the customer among the staff. Although we had a good set of procedures before, our effectiveness is now closely monitored. So, for example, we measured the number of billing enquiries we receive and our response time. We are consciously seeking to improve our performance.'

Since privatisation, Coppack adds, customers demand more from the company. 'As a publicly-owned water authority they gave us more leeway, whereas now they see us as a private company and they expect the job to be done effectively and fast.'

Investor relations

Newly-privatised companies have to realign themselves to the needs of their shareholders. Utilities especially can find that difficult, says Coppack: 'It will take a while for the public service philosophy to work its way out of our system.' But Wessex is working towards this goal. It has appointed an investor relations manager who provides information to actual and potential investors.

'We are now aware of the price of everything we do. This means being far more stringent in some ways. For example, if South West Water had another incident like that at Camelford, Cornwall, when aluminium was accidently deposited in the town's water supply, millions would be wiped off the share price overnight. Incidents like that will be more financially tangible than previously.'

In common with many of Britain's newly privatised organisations, Wessex has a large number of small investors, the outcome of the Conservative government's policy to spread 'popular capitalism'.

Results of the change in status

Says Coppack: 'We learnt a number of lessons from the privatisation process:

- 'Firstly, to plan every step as meticulously as possible and give yourself plenty of time to change the structure and culture of the organisation beforehand. Twelve months is just about long enough.

- 'Secondly, that customers expect much more from a private company than they do from a state-owned corporation.

- 'Thirdly, that a culture change as huge as a move from the public to private sector inevitably takes more time than expected to permeate all levels of the organisation. It has to be backed up by initiatives to educate the workforce, like Wessex '90 and retraining. It is not just a management restructure.'

8

BRITISH AEROSPACE

British Aerospace is one of the largest aerospace organisations in the western world. In July 1979, the government announced its intention to sell the corporation to its employees and the public. Opposition to the move was widespread. When the British Aerospace Bill was debated in the House of Commons in November 1979, the opposition's official spokesman for industry said that a future Labour government would renationalise the company.

Since denationalisation, the company's profits have continued to rise, but it has become more streamlined, made acquisitions away from its core business, and shifted its customer base.

The history of British Aerospace starts in the earliest days of aviation and covers a period of over eighty years. During the First World War, planes such as the Sopwith Camel and the Bristol were built by companies that are now part of British Aerospace. Among the many fighter aircraft built by these companies during the Second World War were the Vickers Supermarine Spitfire, the Hawker Hurricane and the De Havilland Mosquito, one of the fastest and most versatile craft of its time. These aircraft had been made by companies operating in similar fields. In the post-war period, commercial and political pressure brought aircraft companies together. In 1960, Vickers merged with companies such as the Bristol Aeroplane

Company and English Electric to form the British Aircraft Corporation (BAC) in order to compete as aeroplanes and the related equipment became more complicated. The industry's main customer, the Ministry of Defence, wanted to give contracts to a streamlined industrial organisation.

By the 1960s two major players had grown up; Hawker Siddeley, (which included De Havilland Holdings and Folland Aircraft) and BAC. Internationally they were competing in the same market with similar products: for instance, BAC sold the BAC 1–11 against Hawker Siddeley's Trident. As Andrew Wrathall, city relations manager pointed out, the situation was nonsense. 'The companies needed to get together to make better use of valuable engineering resources. They needed to eliminate duplication brought about by the history of mergers of aircraft companies in the UK. Countrywide, for instance, there were several wind tunnels doing the same job, and the industry needed to rationalise.'

The 1977 Aircraft and Shipbuilding Act was a natural progression as well as political dogma. The Act, which brought together companies such as Hawker Siddeley and BAC, enabled British industry to compete against the larger American companies such as McDonnell Douglas. The British Aerospace privatisation cannot be compared with the later privatisation of the Royal Ordnance or the Rover Group, which had long histories as nationalised industries. The former had a history stretching back into the last century and beyond. Andrew Wrathall said: 'When the sell-off came, British Aerospace had been nationalised for under four years. Employees and management had little opportunity to get used to state-owned culture.' The years before nationalisation in 1977 were difficult for the companies, as Andrew Wrathall explained: 'Until the impending issue of nationalisation was resolved, the companies were unwilling to spend money on new products. Programmes such as Trident and 1–11 had been running some years and new products were needed.'

On the eve of the sell-off, the company operated in the civil aircraft sector, the military aircraft sector, and in defence support services to countries like Saudi Arabia. The Dynamics Group produced guided missiles and space systems. It had over 79 000 employees of whom 3300 were overseas, many in Saudi Arabia. Sales in the five years to December 1979 increased from £536 million to £1027 million, and trading profit increased from £43.7 million to £77 million. Military aircraft provided the largest contribution to trading profit. The major part of the Jaguar programme was carried out during this period, while production of the Tornado built up towards the end of this time.

The BAe flotation was small by comparison with other sell-offs, such as Cable and Wireless and British Petroleum, and the later, mammoth sell-offs of water and electricity. The first part came in February 1981 with a fixed-price offer of 51.6 per cent of the company at 150p a share. The government retained 48 per cent since it was a major defence contractor. Proceeds of £100 million from this sale were put back into the company as a capital injection. In May 1985 the government sold its remaining stake at 375p a share. It was left with no residual shareholding other than a single 'golden share'. The second sale included a 'rights issue' as a combined share offer which raised a further £187.5 million for the company.

To encourage employee involvement in the company in 1991, staff were given preferential share allocations. This was a matching share allocation, which meant that for every share they bought, they were given the same number free. Andrew Wrathall explained: 'The aim was to give staff a direct involvement in the performance of the company, although the numbers of staff owning shares fell very rapidly.'

After privatisation British Aerospace set about the long process of rationalisation. At that point there were thirty British manufacturing bases and eight airfields. The company was duplicating resources on a grand scale. In the years 1982–86, six plants were closed. After the 1977 nationalisation, another management layer had been added. The company was split into two distinct sections, Aircraft and Dynamics, with a head office and board of directors above that. The new organisation had only been superficial, since the divisions within the sections were still identifiable as the old companies. Even though the former De Havilland organisation in Hatfield and Chester was now part of a nationalised British Aerospace, for example, the sites still had the same facilities and management structure as formerly.

Facilities, too, needed to be reorganised. In 1981 the company owned eleven wind tunnels and used eight flight test centres. By 1988, rationalisation was well under way, with management streamlined into Military Aircraft, Dynamics, Commercial Aircraft and Space Divisions.

The source of the company's aerospace business has now shifted, with more emphasis on overseas contracts and decreased reliance on UK government contracts. Before privatisation, over 80 per cent of British Aerospace business was defence business. Now it is only 40 per cent. Andrew Wrathall explained: 'We produced a high proportion of our equipment for the British forces. There was little chance of us growing as a government supplier, so after privatisation we deliberately became more export oriented.' Previously British Aerospace had worked alongside the Ministry of Defence to develop systems to meet their requirements. Export was a sideline — the Tornado, for example, was only exported well into the programme for the UK forces. Following privatisation, however, the company began to develop products such as the Laserfire air defence system and the Hawk 200 combat aircraft specifically for overseas markets.

Privatisation also cleared the way for major investment on the commercial aircraft side, one of the world's fastest growing industries. 'The privatisation made management sit down and look very carefully at where the business was going,' said Andrew Wrathall. 'The company was profitable throughout the nationalisation period, but after the sell-off management were perhaps more aware of their responsibility to their shareholders. Decisions had to be of high quality. Looking at the way the aircraft industry was moving, they decided that returns could be enhanced by investment in commercial aircraft programmes and by becoming much more export oriented. We ploughed an enormous amount of money into the commercial sector in the early '80s with little return until 1989.' In common with many denationalised companies, British Aerospace has felt the need to become more growth and profit oriented. 'For shareholders to be content, we have to move forward and keep up a dynamic which will outstrip the returns of investment in other spheres, such as the bank.'

Although the underlying trend has been a declining employee population since the sell-off, the number of people employed by the company has grown. British Aerospace employed only 79 000 people when it was first floated, now the total working population is 125 000. The additional people came from acquisitions such as the Rover Group, Ballast Nedem and Royal Ordnance. Sales per employee have gone up dramatically, and turnover has increased eight times.

'In the mid-1980s', Andrew Wrathall said, 'it was a hands on business managed from the centre.' Now the separate businesses are autonomous and required to provide a reasonable rate of return for the cash that is provided by the centre. The group of companies do draw some mutual benefits, however. The group shares manpower and technology. Computers are networked. High-flyers are found top appointments in other parts of the organisation.

Management and shareholders now have a long-term faith in the future of the business and have concentrated on maximising efficiency. For example, in 1986 the then chief executive, Sir Reynold Lygo, initiated a drive to reduce manufacturing costs by a third. As a result, the final assembly time of the Harrier II, for instance, was reduced from twenty-seven to twenty weeks. The single most expensive item on the four-engined BAe 146 regional jet airliner were the engines. At any one time, there were ten weeks' worth of engines on site. Today British Aerospace only has two weeks' worth of engines on the premises.

'It is not just building the machines with fewer people,' explained Andrew Wrathall. 'We are more disciplined at taking parts into the programmes. We are more cost conscious now. We practise inventory control and put the most expensive items on last and all the cheap and cheerful bits on first. Our main customer is no longer the Ministry of Defence, so we have to be internationally competitive.' He added: 'In fact, our cost improvement programme has been so successful, we have achieved our target reduction in three years, and not the five originally planned.'

9

REPSOL

Oscar Fanjul
Chairman and CEO of Repsol, SA

The 1980s saw the development of privatisation worldwide. This process has taken place on different continents and in industrialised and developing countries. It has been promoted by conservative and socialist governments alike. Privatisation has been the central tenet of certain governments' policy, such as Margaret Thatcher's. In Eastern Europe, it seems that the privatisation process will continue throughout the 1990s, intensifying as its component countries move away from a centralised economy.

There are two common features in the process. Firstly a disillusionment about the state's capability to produce in an efficient manner. Secondly a revaluation of the market as a mechanism for resource allocation. At both the micro- and macro-econonomic levels, theories and expectations that arose after the Second World War about the state's role as stabiliser and allocator have been called into question. These were the theories and expectations that inspired not just social-democratic governments like those in Britain and Scandinavia, but also influenced the thinking of conservative governments in France and other European countries.

However, the privatisation process has varied from country to country. The reasons for privatisation, the methods, prevailing economic and social restrictions and variation in the objectives pursued have often differed radically. The study that follows is an attempt to analyse the main privatisation carried out in Spain, emphasising those elements that distinguish it from other European experiences. It will also examine the way in which common problems were tackled, look at specific Spanish problems and detail the privatisation of a major oil company, Repsol.

Background: The Public Industry Sector in Spain

The Spanish public industry sector developed in 1939 after the Civil War. The Instituto Nacional de Industria (National Industry Institute – INI) set up in 1941, took Mussolini's Italian Istituto per Ricostruzione Industriale (IRI) as its direct model. INI is a state agency that has acted as a holding company for a large number of companies. These firms span most industrial sectors including mining, iron and steel, shipyards, vehicles, food and electronics, transport, electricity generation and distribution.

The origins of nationalised companies in Spain lie thus in a politically conservative system and are not associated with nationalisation movements, such as those experienced in the rest of Europe after the Second World War. The argument that was used in Spain to justify the creation and development of this part of the public sector was the lack of private initiative to industrialise Spain, a lack of initiative evidenced by the absence of capital and of agents ready to *take risks*. Deep down there was a lack of trust in the capability of the free market to promote economic growth. At that point, the Spanish authorities believed the state could introduce a greater economic logic because it cared about collective welfare and not just individual profit.

Although it was initially planned that state-owned companies would act only in cases where private initiatives did not exist, once the INI was created it developed into an organisation with much wider objectives. Some of the many objectives pursued by state-owned companies since 1941 until the Seventies have included increasing the degree of competition, compensating for regional imbalances and having state ownership in strategic sectors such as defence. The number of state-owned companies also grew through the sale of loss-making companies to the public sector.

However, the public sector did not become a large proportion of economic activity. Table 9.1 shows the relatively small importance of Spanish state-owned companies in comparison with the rest of Europe. The economic events that occurred in the 1970s had a major effect on state-owned companies, especially on their financial results and the role that was allotted to them as far as economic and industrial policy was concerned.

The Origin and Nature of Spanish Privatisations

The Spanish economy underwent rapid industrialisation and growth in the 1960s, then during the following decade experienced major inflation and stagnation. The first oil crisis coincided with the end of the old political system and the development of a transition towards a democratic system. Whilst suffering from the first oil shock, Spain had to draw up a new political constitution, develop trade unions, and reorganise its political life. In this context, the Spanish economy suffered an acute crisis from 1973 to 1985: unemployment rose from 2.7 per cent to a peak of 21.6 per cent and the current account balance fell from a surplus of Ptas31.8 billion to a deficit of Ptas160.2 billion. The crisis had a particularly severe impact on industry. To ease social pressure, conservative

Table 9.1   *The importance of state-owned companies in Spain and Europe*

Size	Spain	EC Average
State-owned/Total employment	5%	10%
State-owned/Total investment	10%	20%
Gross value of state-owned companies/ GDP (excluding agriculture)	8%	12%
Gross Added Value by sector: (as a percentage of GDP)		
· Energy	29%	70%
· Transport and Communications	45%	70%
· Banking and Insurance	10%	30%

Source: *Statistics Yearbook of the European State-owned Companies Centre (1987)*

governments agreed to nationalise companies on the brink of bankruptcy, which accentuated the public debt.

The Partido Socialista Obrero Español (Spanish Socialist Workers' Party – PSOE) secured the first absolute majority in the elections of October 1982. By this time, the new Spanish government's economic policy was characterised by the search for macroeconomic stability and deregulation, as well as market liberalisation in the micro-economy. Unlike the French, the Spanish did not pursue nationalisation and demand expansion, but followed the Australian and New Zealand model.

For state-owned companies, this meant, first, a drastic abandonment of the old policy of nationalising bankrupt private companies in order to protect their owners and their employees and, second, the beginning of a process of selling state-owned companies. This process has never been explicitly defined or formed part of a specific privatisation programme. It is very important to understand this latter characteristic of Spanish privatisations, which sets them apart from other European experiences. Although they actually occurred in the same period, there were very important differences between the Spanish process of privatisation and those that were developed in the United Kingdom, France and other European countries, both in the justification of the process and the way in which it was implemented.

The Spanish socialist government was not dismantling a welfare state. It was building it up in order to bring its social services closer to European Community standards. It did not seek to reduce union power, but to help to consolidate their role and power through legislative development and financial aid. It did not use privatisation to finance tax cuts. In fact, privatisation has not been included in the policy programme of any government, nor has it been the subject of ideological or political discussions.

So, why have major privatisations of state-owned companies taken place in Spain? Firstly to cut back on the budgetary load of loss-making companies. For example, public holdings in the car company SEAT and the industrial vehicles company ENASA were sold to multi-national groups. The scale and technology required by this industry made it very difficult for such companies to survive independently. A number of other companies in other sectors are included in this category, such as hotel, textile and travel companies. These were sold to Spanish or foreign private companies, who were willing to meet the challenge of revitalising and managing them.

Second, there were other profitable companies, where the state owned all or almost all of the shares. Where there was no reason for such a high holding, an increased private stake and greater compliance with market rules were considerd appropriate.

Spain was negotiating its entry into the European Community at the time and Spanish industry was preparing itself for increased competition. Access to the EC and later the Single European Market were regarded as serious challenges in

Spain. Companies felt that there would be a competitive environment which would force them to be more efficient.

For a company like Repsol full state ownership was considered a hindrance, and, for this reason, its management proposed the company should be privatised.

The government fully supported the proposal for various reasons. Firstly, it made a commitment to pay higher dividends when Repsol was listed on the Stock Exchange. Secondly, Repsol's privatisation was consistent with government policy of adjustment to the EC and market liberalisation. Finally, the government knew the difficulties a state-owned company faced if it was to become efficient. It wanted to help Repsol overcome some of these drawbacks. Apart from this, the oil sector, to which the company belonged, was becoming increasingly competitive as the government rapidly deregulated it.

The Public Oil Sector in Spain: Campsa, INH and Repsol

The State founded Campsa in 1928 to create a national oil company as had been done, or was to be done, by governments in Britain, France and Italy. Campsa was born amid strong opposition from other Spanish companies and foreign multinationals. Although it never became the vertically integrated company it set out to be, it gained a monopoly position in the distribution and marketing of oil products.

Until recently, the Spanish oil sector was under strict regulation. The State set the prices, authorised the setting-up of refineries, restricted imports and so on. Within this framework, there was no justification or opportunity to develop an integrated oil company. Nevertheless, in this climate, independent exploration, refining and petrochemical companies developed. Ownership of these companies has been variable. They were either owned by Spanish or foreign capital. Some companies were private and others were partially or completely state-owned.

Two events made the State reconsider its oil policy. First, Spain was heavily dependent upon imported energy and the oil crisis of the 1970s demonstrated the importance of an efficient oil industry. Secondly, Spain was seeking to enter the EEC, which meant that existing regulations had to disappear and free competition be introduced.

In 1981 the Instituto Nacional de Hidrocarburos (INH) was created to incorporate State interests in the oil, chemical and gas industry. This included different types of company, including two exploration and production companies, two in refining and four in chemicals. See Table 9.2 for INH's structure after all the different companies operating in the same field were merged in 1985–86.

INH was the first step in the co-ordinated planning and management of a major basket of Spanish oil assets. In 1987, INH became an integrated oil company with the same characteristics as the competition. This required two measures. First, it meant converting an agency into a company. Eight large companies were merged, and homogeneous management, planning control and a single corporate identity were introduced. Repsol was born in 1987. Its name was not new but was taken from a well known brand of lubricants within the group. Tables 9.3 and 9.4 show the new organisation of INH and Repsol. Secondly, normalisation demanded that the company should no longer have just one owner, the state, but be quoted on the stock market like other companies of Repsol's size. How the 1989 flotation was carried out will be addressed in the following sections.

Preparation for Repsol's privatisation took several years. The company had to be financially reorganised and its profitability increased so that it could be sold at a fair price. Profits grew during this period. At the same time Repsol undertook a number of corporate image and product campaigns, to make itself better known than its former subsidiaries. Within two years Repsol was one of the best known companies in Spain.

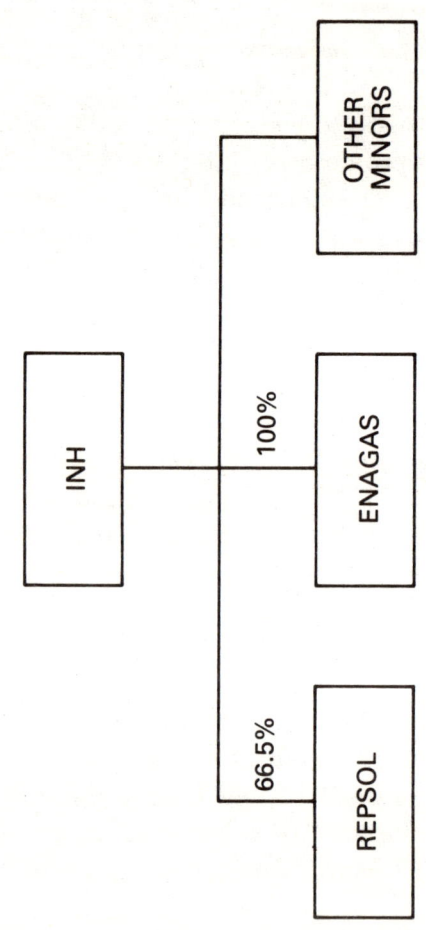

Table 9.2 INH Corporate Structure

Table 9.3 Corporate structure prior to the creation of REPSOL (Principal Companies)

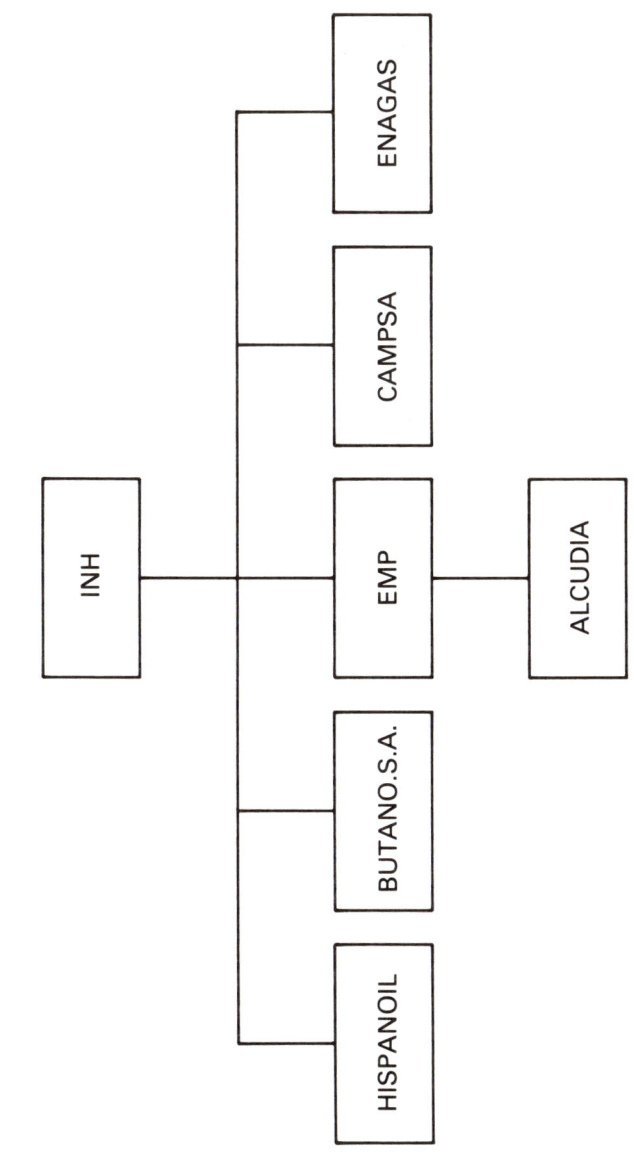

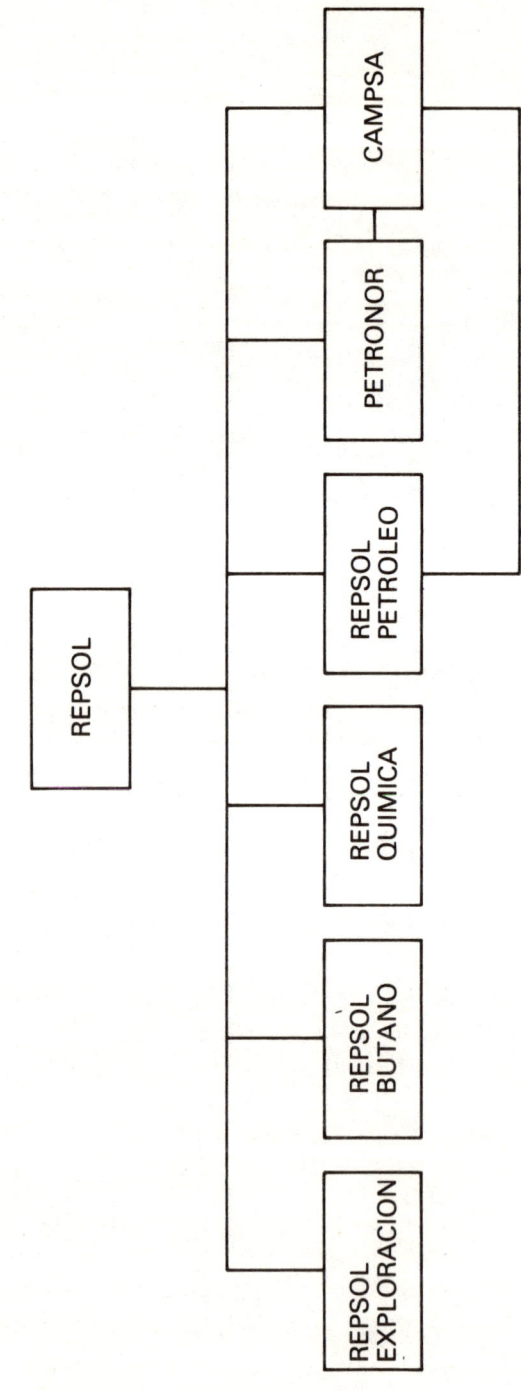

Table 9.4 Corporate Structure of REPSOL

The Privatisation Strategy

In 1989, Repsol was a new company operating in an industry subject to a deregulation process and growing competition. It decided to take advantage of privatisation preparations to help its consolidation strategy. Going public was used to achieve two objectives: firstly, to improve the company's asset structure and secondly, to improve the company's relationship with its employees, customers, suppliers, and marketing channels in general. In short, the privatisation process was used to improve the company's efficiency and competitivity. For example, core shareholders were chosen for the assets they could contribute. BBV, the top-ranking Spanish bank, became Repsol's leading shareholder by contributing a majority holding in three companies. One of these was the largest and most modern Spanish refinery in which Repsol already had a minority stake. The others were a speciality chemical comany and a shipping business. The Mexican oil firm, Pemex, became the other main shareholder. Customers of the former INH companies covered a wide sector of Spanish society, and they were all potential shareholders in Repsol.

The need for privatisation was explained in great detail and over a long period so that it would not be criticised by political parties or the unions. A special information programme was aimed at the company's workers. They were able to buy discount shares on credit to foster commitment in the workforce. Service station dealers and commercial distributors were covered by a similar scheme.

A full-scale advertising campaign was carried out in two phases. First, well before the flotation came the attempt to make the company well known. Second, the public were invited to buy shares in the newly famous company. Various polls and surveys identified the company as one of the most admired for the quality of its management and one of the most favoured by university graduates looking for their first job. In short, the process of going public was used to improve the quality of company assets, to consolidate its commercial

177

position and to improve relations with suppliers, distributors and the public in general.

Size of the Operation

As Tables 9.5, 9.6 and 9.7 show the initial public offering of Repsol was double the size of any previous operation carried out on the Spanish capital markets.

The operation would obviously have been simpler if a smaller proportion of the capital had been placed on the stock market, but the amount chosen seemed to be the lowest limit if private shareholders were to enter the company in a real rather

Table 9.5   Volume of initial public offerings in Spain, 1986–88

	Ptas × million
1986	19,840
1987	80,572
1988	126,417
Repsol (1989)	135,000

Table 9.6   Main initial public offerings in Spain, 1986–89

Company	Amount (Ptas × million)	Shareholders
GESA (1986)	8,205	13,600
ACESA (1987)	47,000	58,000
ENDESA (1988)	74,200	70,000
REPSOL (1989)	135,000	380,000

Table 9.7   Main recent public offerings, 1987–1989

Company	US$ × million
British Petroleum (1987)	12.571
British Steel (1988)	4.672
Compagnie Financière de Suez (1987)	2.539
Société Générale (1987)	1.919
Compagnie Générale d'Électricité (1987)	1.742
Compagnie Financière de Paris (1987)	1.391
Veba (1987)	1.375
British Airways (1987)	1.364
Repsol (1989)	1.100
Viag (1988)	0.871
Eurotunnel (1987)	0.741
Endeas (1988)	0.651
DSM (1989)	0.614
Aachener und Muenchener (1987)	0.402
Mediobanca (1988)	0.400
DAF (1989)	0.384
Barclays (1987)	0.383
Yves Saint Laurent (1989)	0.520
Enimont (1989)	0.849
British Water (1989)	8.280

than a symbolic way. At the same time, a reduction in the volume placed would have meant an increase in the average cost of the share offer. In addition, throughout the flotation period, the October 1987 crash was still in the minds of many.

This made it considerably more difficult to gain access to capital markets. When Repsol originally began to toy with the idea of privatisation, financial analysts thought it might be difficult to achieve. In practice, with meticulous preparation and sufficient explanation to the general public, the absorption capacity of the markets was much greater than previously thought.

Design of the Placing

The size of the operation was a basic factor in the type of placing designed. Other determinants included the fact that it was a state-owned company, and a large number of potential shareholders were also customers. It was therefore necessary to guarantee a placing with specific characteristics. A key restriction was the small size of the Spanish capital market in relation to any reasonable capitalisation value for Repsol. The market was also characterised by certain dubious practices that were inappropriate for a modern market or for the concept of market in itself. Institutional investment had little importance. No developed pension funds existed. This meant that the shares had to be sold in a different way from what had hapened in other countries. These characteristics had a decisive influence on the design of the placing.

A wide shareholder base: the retail tranche

The operation's size and the absence of major institutional investors meant we had to resort to a high number of potential shareholders. Since a company of the importance of Repsol was involved, it seemed sensible for the share offer to be public, so that anyone could buy. This made it different from the majority of Spanish placings, which have been private.

Institutional tranche

The institutional tranche was targeted at insurance companies, pension funds and mutual funds. Share applications
with a value greater than Ptas40 million (around £200 000)
were considered.

Liquidity and transparency

Particular care was taken to ensure adequate liquidity and
transparency of the share price. Repsol started the quotation as
soon as possible after allocation to ensure that the share would
be very liquid and behave stably. For operational reasons, the
Spanish stock market did not admit Repsol into the 'continuous market', which had just started operating[1]. Nevertheless, the objectives remained fully guaranteed through the
listing of the shares on the New York Stock Exchange (NYSE)
and SEAQ.

Initial share behaviour

The share offer to the public was developed over a limited
period of time: two weeks. There were two reasons for this:
firstly, if the time interval were not limited, there would be no
reason for taking the step of buying, as the decision could
always be delayed until a later date. Secondly, this interval
must be sufficiently short to be an assumable risk for the
underwriters: on a fixed date they signed the underwriting

---

[1]Until 1989, every share was traded on the Spanish stock markets in an open
voice auction system, for a time of ten minutes. In July 1989, an electronic
trading system (CATS) was put in function, allowing the shares included to
be traded from 10:00 to 17:00.

agreement by which they are committed to buying all the shares offered at a certain price; therefore, the more time lapses, the greater is the risk of a significant fluctuation in stock market prices that could lead them to incur losses.

International tranche and listing in New York

Both the volume of the operation and the need for stable investors and assets made it advisable to design an international tranche. The international offering was in great demand. It also meant that Repsol had to be on the alert since these investors would have their own specialised analysis departments backing investment decisions. The analysts would look closely at the company, its strategy and its performance.

The NYSE was, in fact, able to guarantee additional demand after placing. This had already occurred for Endesa, one of the big Spanish utilities, when it went public. Equally, the US stock market seemed essential to guaranteeing the share's liquidity, as could be seen from the first day of the quotation.

The requirement for a listing on the NYSE are stricter than for the Spanish stock market. Compliance with the requirements of the US listing constituted a demanding challenge for the company and a considerable guarantee for shareholders. Both these factors appear to us to be highly important and to lie at the root of the decision to privatise. Auditors, lawyers, financial analysts and Repsol collaborators worked to get the company fit for inspection by the Security Exchange Commission.

The following were important features of the international offering:

- A syndicate was formed with a regional structure to create competition among the three regions, United States, Japan, and the rest of the world, to obtain shares.

- There was no Global Manager. Repsol was a co-ordinator among the three regions.

- The Japanese tranche was frozen: The underwriters were committed to holding the shares in the country for at least one year.

- The market was basically institutional.

Results

Table 9.8 shows the results of the placing by tranches and comparing them with those of Endesa, the biggest previous flotation.

The retail tranche was very important for Repsol (see Table 9.9, page 184) Repsol placed more shares on the Spanish Stock Market than any previous flotation. Only three other Spanish companies had as many shareholders as Repsol (more than 380 000). There are two aspects of this that are worth analysing in more detail.

Table 9.8 Distribution by tranches

Tranches	Endesa (Ptas × million)	%	Repsol (Ptas × million)	%
Domestic	46,200	62	86,700	64
Retail	*36,960*	*37*	*75,310*	*56*
Institutional	*9,240*	*25*	*11,390*	*8*
International	28,000	38	48,875	38
TOTAL	74,200	100	135,575	100

Table 9.9   Number of shareholders

Company	Shareholders
Telefonica	700,000
Banco Bilbao Vizcaya (BBV)	410,061
REPSOL	380,018
Banco de Santander	365,565
Banco Hispano Americano	292,017
Banco Espanol de Credito (Banesto)	167,643
Banco Popular	97,569

Pro rata allocation

The shares were almost three times oversubscribed. The existence of oversubscription raises the problem of the pro-rata allocation, or the distribution of a limited quantity of available shares. In the case of Repsol, the procedure that was followed (previously agreed with the 52 underwriting institutions) was the one legally set down for the issuing of fixed income issues, both from the Treasury and from private investors.

Small investors benefited since the average investment was Ptas167 000 and the maximum Ptas413 000. Specifically, 350 000 shareholders accounted for more than 40 per cent of the applications, a high percentage when compared with the major British and French privatisations.

Logistics

Particular attention was paid to the logistic development of the operation because of the time constraint imposed by being quoted in New York, as well as the wish to carry out the operation to defend new shareholders' interests. Repsol aimed to minimise the days between the share subscription closing, the announcement of the allocation and the moment at which the shares were quoted. All records were broken. As Table 9.10 (page 186) shows, only three days elapsed between the end of the subscription period and the announcement of the allocation, when the usual lapse in Spain is more than twenty days. The shares were quoted within five days as against the forty-day period that is normal in Spain. In addition, shares were paid for after the allocation, to the advantage of underwriters and investors.

Conclusion

Going public for staff and managers at Repsol had certain significant implications. One of the most positive, in my opinion, was the introduction of greater discipline in the way we take short- and long-term decisions. Today, whenever a decision is discussed, we take into account its likely assessment by the capital markets. This means that more importance is attached to the impact of a decision on short- and long-term results. It is said that the stock market is biased towards the short-term. There may be some truth in this, but we started off with an almost complete absence of external control and the external monitoring has proved beneficial for us.

Today more than sixty institutions follow the company, publish research about it and assess the quality of our management team. It is difficult to undervalue the importance of this assessment.

Because of the degree of efficiency demanded by the New York Stock Exchange, our decision to be quoted there has been as important as privatisation itself.

Table 9.10 Logistics of Spanish initial public offerings

Issuer	Placing period	Days from closure until result announced	until start of quoting
Acerinox	July 86	77	92
Acesa	February 87	15	91
Aforasa	December 87	45	69
Amper	May 86	21	56
Aumar	June 87	15	22
B. Atlántico	June 87	85	93
Ceselsa	March 87	7	42
Elosua	November 87	25	58
Ence	February 88	37	44
Ercros	October 87	6	17
Erpo	February 87	6	10
Gas Madrid	November 87	10	15
Gesa	October 86	10	76
Hullas	May 87	18	31
Prosegur	February 87	6	43
Vidrala	June 87	22	81
Jumberca	May 88	6	56
CAE	May 88	5	16
Pascual Hnos.	May 88	25	30
Prima	August 88	17	30
	AVERAGE	23	48
REPSOL		3	5

10

CABLE AND WIRELESS

Lord Sharp of Grimsdyke, CBE,
Chairman and Chief Executive

Cable and Wireless came into being in 1929 through the merger of many privately-owned British companies that had been among the pioneers of international telecommunications, in the nineteenth century by submarine cable and in the twentieth century by radio or 'wireless'. The business remained in private hands from 1866 to 1946, when it was nationalised.

During the 1930s, when Cable and Wireless was suffering from the depression of international trade, increasing competition from foreign-owned wireless telegraph services, and the expansion of pure telephony, the company initiated a policy of pursuing franchises to operate telecommunications in many foreign countries, and introducing a broader range of telephony. It was during this period that Cable and Wireless gained the franchises to run Bahrain's domestic and international services (in 1931) and Hong Kong's external wireless services (in 1938); Cable and Wireless had been operating Hong Kong's telegraph services since the late nineteenth century. These two franchises were to provide the business launch-pad for the company's return to the private sector in 1981.

At the outbreak of the Second World War, Cable and Wireless owned the world's most extensive international cable and radio network, and operated international telecommunication services in all the main Commonwealth countries, including the United Kingdom. The company remained in the private sector throughout the war when its staff provided the allied powers with an invaluable worldwide communications service, which has been well documented in *The Thin Blue Line*. However, by the end of the war, certain Commonwealth countries had indicated their desire to have direct control over their external telecommunications.

In 1945, the government agreed to the recommendation of a London conference that the governments of Great Britain, Australia, Canada, India and South Africa should operate their external telecommunications independently. Following the Cable and Wireless Act of 1946, the company's share capital was acquired by the Treasury; Cable and Wireless was to continue under state control for the next thirty-five years.

Although Cable and Wireless operated under the companies Act, it was essentially a nationalised undertaking: all board appointments and remuneration of directors had to be determined by the minister responsible; its investment programme had to be approved by the Treasury; its general policy and operations had to be regularly reviewed by the department concerned and, occasionally, by Parliamentary committee.

During those thirty-five years, the Treasury's attitude to the performance of Cable and Wireless could be characterised as one of benign neglect. As long as the company was making reasonable profits, which it did, the Treasury could concentrate on the huge losses being incurred by other nationalised industries. The monitoring of the performance and policies of Cable and Wireless by Parliament, as representative of shareholders' interests, was confined to a two-hour review by a Select Committee every three to four years. On the other hand, the freedom to invest and to change strategic direction was very much circumscribed. Any project over £10m required Treasury approval: this regulation clearly acted as a brake on management initiative and enterprise. Any attempt to change the company's strategic thrust became enmeshed in the problems of ministerial and government bureaucracy.

There were two major technological developments in telecommunications during the 1950s and 1960s which stimulated the growth of international telephone and telex traffic and helped to keep Cable and Wireless comfortably afloat. The first trans-oceanic coaxial telephone cable was laid under the Atlantic ocean in 1956, and the first geostationary telecommunications space satellite came into operation in 1965.

Although Cable and Wireless succeeded in keeping abreast of the new technology and invested heavily in new equipment in Hong Kong, Bahrain and the Caribbean during the 1960s and the 1970s, the company was, inevitably, engineering-led and had no strategy at all to steer a course through the choppy waters of post-war politics. Many former colonies, having gained their independence, could afford to take advantage of the new cheap satellite technology and, already highly trained by Cable and Wireless engineers, they duly decided to take over the operation of their own telecommunications. The same loss of franchises occurred in South America, where Cable and Wireless used to hold a unique position.

Cable and Wireless was still able to rest on its laurels because many of the territories where the company operated experienced a period of substantial economic growth, which was reflected in an increasing volume of traffic (notably in Hong Kong and Bahrain during the 1970s). The main challenge facing the Cable and Wireless board was how to employ surplus staff, caused by the shrinkage of business in South America, and create 'jobs for the boys' elsewhere. Their response was to look for businesses in the United States and Europe which were not related to the core business. These businesses had no strategic relevance but had just enough relevance to satisfy the minister. Unsurprisingly, these marginal businesses in the maintenance and manufacture of equipment made very little profit compared with Cable and Wireless's historic business of operating international tele-

communications, and the future of the company looked deci-
dedly bleak by the end of the Labour Party's term of office in
1979.

Some may argue that it would have made no difference to
Cable and Wireless whether it was nationalised or not during
those thirty-five years — it was subject to the ebb and flow of
international trading streams, and the government provided a
protective cover against the chill winds of change. My own
view is that the experience of Cable and Wireless after privatisation demonstrates clearly that government ownership had
only a negative effect on the company. If Cable and Wireless
were a lame duck then it should have been allowed to die. As
it continued to make profits *despite* state control, it can be
assumed that the company was very much a going concern
which only needed the freedom to stretch its wings.

My predecessor as chairman of Cable and Wireless gave a
classic example of the way in which ministers interpret their
responsibility for a nationalised enterprise and the restraint
that imposes on management expertise. Giving evidence before a Select Committee of the House of Commons in 1978, he
said that, at the time of the last review in 1974, the Government had imposed restrictions on the company's development
in the UK. They did not insist that the company should stop
doing anything, but they did say that Cable and Wireless
should not pursue the business 'actively' (*sic*) in the UK
because of the sensitivity to the interests of the Post Office,
which was responsible for telecommunications at that time.
After further approaches in 1974, the then secretary of state
gave approval to a limited extension of Cable and Wireless
activities, saying that the relaxation was on the understanding
that the company, and I quote 'consult the Department about
any major expansion or developments of any expansion which
might be politically or financially sensitive.'

This is a vivid description of the dead hand of bureaucracy
stifling any spark of initiative. Cable and Wireless could
certainly not have taken the advantage it has of the liberalisation in the UK market, through its subsidiary Mercury Com-

munications, with that kind of political intervention. It would be like trying to win at table tennis with both hands tied behind your back.

The sporting metaphor is a useful one because it brings in the element of competition, a factor which is noticeably lacking in any monopolist's view of the world. The idea that the quality of telecommunications service provided to the public would improve beyond all recognition if healthy competition was introduced was unthinkable to the champions of nationalisation in the late 1970s. Even the Conservative government of 1979 could not conceive of introducing competition without first consulting British Telecom — something which seems absurd today.

When I was appointed chairman and chief executive of Cable and Wireless in 1981 to lead the company through the experience of privatisation, I had already experienced the problem of relations between government and publicly-owned industry, from both sides of the fence. I was a civil servant in the Ministry of Power in 1948 and I was involved in the civil service's first enquiry into the efficiency and operation of a nationalised industry (Electricity Supply 1955–56). Until I returned briefly to government in 1980, my career had been in the textile and chemical industries — private companies, but large enough to attract the attention of governments. I also kept in touch with the problems of nationalised industry through my membership of the Central Electricity Generating Board. During that time, I discovered that the general problems of nationalised industry management defy general, dogmatic solutions. In theory, a responsible minister acts as the custodian of the national interest and the representative of the shareholders. In practice, ministerial relations with nationalised corporations are confused and arbitrary.

Ministers cannot forget that they have a duty and a loyalty to their colleagues in government and its broad social and economic policies. The accounts of the nationalised industries and other publicly owned enterprises are an important component of the government's finances and as such are vulnerable: vulnerable to changes in the many economic variables which shape the way in which different governments arrange their financial affairs; vulnerable to changes in policy; and vulnerable to changes in governments themselves. Ministers find it difficult to be committed to the long term. As the average 'life' of a minister is about two years under any administration, the chairman of a nationalised corporation is often faced with developing new relationships with new ministers who may well have differing ideas about their responsibilities.

The result of this continually shifting scene is that, despite all the thorough and resource-consuming traditional five-year plans, which are the formal basis of ministerial involvement in the affairs of nationalised industries, it is impossible for the business and political cycles to be kept in phase with one another.

Parliament's understandable concern about the public accountability of nationalised industries is bound up with the recurrent failure to find a satisfactory standard means of measuring their performance. The same anxiety afflicts the corporation itself: Cable and Wireless directors and managers were never certain about the financial objective which they were required to meet. Even though they operated under the Companies Act, their freedom to manage was always more apparent than real: they were caretakers rather than directors.

As well as having the right of veto over capital investment programmes and individual projects, ministers also approved appointments to the board, and salary scales had to be related to the civil service system. Directors' salaries were kept down by ministers. At one point in 1977 the whole executive board tendered their resignations. In fact the resignations did not take place: the situation was fudged by changing the titles of some directors in order to give them an increase in salary. Many staff retired at fifty-five because it was of no financial benefit for them to continue until they were sixty. Talent was being dissipated by uniformity and conformity in salaries — rewards were not related to performance.

In 1979, a new Conservative government was elected, committed to the withdrawal of state intervention in industry and the free market philosophy. Cable and Wireless was chosen as an early candidate for privatisation in the government's programme because it had already experienced a long history in the private sector and, by virtue of the company's low profile in Britain, its return to private ownership would cause few ripples. What made this privatisation different was the sector: telecommunications. The new government had an unusually clear-cut policy of telecommunications liberalisation.

In July 1980, the secretary of state for industry made a policy statement outlining the government's plans for liberalising both the telecommunication and postal markets and for privatising Cable and Wireless. From July 1980 to July 1981, the mechanics for deregulation were established and, within government, the way was cleared to issue a licence for an alternative, privately-owned telecommunications network (Mercury Communications Ltd), and the possibility of privatising British Telecom came under consideration.

On my arrival at Cable and Wireless head office in London, I found a very comfortable board. None of the board papers seemed to have any bottom-line implications. The company was a highly centralised organisation; no one in the overseas regions had any true concept of profit and loss. The regional picture emerged only at the centre, which meant that decision-making was highly centralised, too. It was equivalent to the way the Admiralty worked in the seventeenth and eighteenth centuries when they used to send barrels of rum from the quartermaster's stores to Jamaica.

In those early days, there was a good deal of resistance to any change at all — from within Cable and Wireless, despite its early history. Visions had been blinkered by many years of state control. The extent of Cable and Wireless's commercial freedom was perhaps the most contentious issue, both within government and the company: it was thought that governments overseas would not trust their franchises to a private company, though in reality hardly any government at all objected on these grounds. It was further stated that Cable and Wireless could not be privatised without disrupting the company's position in Hong Kong and Bahrain, the two largest contributors to group profits. Participation in the establishment of Mercury was also seen as a considerable challenge.

The first, and perhaps most important, consequence of the decision to privatise Cable and Wireless was to instil a new spirit of 'can do and must do' in its management, who were galvanised by the urgent need to meet tight timetables. Problems, however difficult, were there to be solved and solved constructively, and, for the first time in years, with an eye on the bottom line.

Our immediate tasks were: to introduce new accounting systems to satisfy City prospectus requirements; to restructure the business in Hong Kong and Bahrain; to decentralise management; and to define a new corporate strategy. The strategy had to include the company's re-entry into the UK as a fully-fledged operator, in a market already dominated by a publicly-owned enterprise, British Telecom.

The introduction of new accounting and financial systems was not easy, since it entailed a major reorganisation of the way accounts were made up and a disaggregation of activities. This could not be achieved overnight, but a minimum of change was necessary to satisfy the prospectus requirements. The changes in our accounting systems, introduced in 1980–81, were only the beginning of a process which is still continuing as we enhance and refine our accounting and mangement information systems today. The accounts in our 1981 prospectus are relatively primitive when compared with the set of accounts we submitted in 1989 to the Securities Exchange Commission in New York for our American Depositary Receipts quotation. The real point here is that privatisation made it essential for the company to establish detailed financial controls and a reliable overview of its assets. From this new base, we were able to forge an active financial strategy to exploit Cable and Wireless's unique position within the telecommunications world.

The restructuring of Cable and Wireless in Hong Kong and Bahrain was an important learning experience for the company. What was considered impossible within the old frame-work — the conversion of Cable and Wireless interests from local branches, accountable to no one except London collea-gues, into properly accountable, Companies Act compa-nies — now had to be done.

The complex negotiations with government and financial advisers within a tight schedule proved a formative expe-rience for the best managers within the company (some of whom are now among our leading directors) and created a new company capability to act decisively in seizing business opportunities and to turn potential threats into opportunities. Cable and Wireless was already showing its mettle.

At the same time as the company was going through these necessary internal changes, it was actively having to respond to the government's wish to see network competition intro-duced in the UK. Negotiations over a licence for Mercury were undertaken under the most difficult circumstances — all negotiations with government were subject to consultation with British Telecom, which was then a fully-owned govern-ment enterprise. The reference to Mercury in the 1981 Cable and Wireless prospectus is highly tentative, reflecting these difficulties:

HM Government has agreed in principle to grant a licence to the Company to permit a consortium to provide and operate a telecommunications network for the United Kingdom, to be known as Mercury. Discussions are taking place between HM Government, the Company and British Telecom on the terms upon which Mercury may be permitted interconnec-tion with British Telecom's public network and a secure international outlet. The Directors believe that it is essential for Mercury to achieve full technical and operational con-trol of an international outlet and interconnection with British Telecom's public network if Mercury is to proceed.

In November 1981, Cable and Wireless was privatised. Fifty per cent of the shares were offered for sale by the government and, under the prospectus governing the issue, it was made clear that the company would henceforth be as free as any other company in the private sector to conduct its own affairs. Further sales of government shares were made in November 1983 and December 1985. Today, the government not only holds a 'golden share' in Cable and Wireless but has also ensured that no one individual can hold more than 15 per cent of the company. The second sale of Cable and Wireless shares in 1983 offered shares to the company's employees on attractive terms when the success of privatisation was already visible in the figures. Furthermore, the threat of competition was already beginning to affect the behaviour of British Telecom, in favour of the customer.

The immediate effect of freedom from government bureaucracy and specifically Treasury control meant that Cable and Wireless was enabled independently to develop a corporate strategy and, most importantly, to implement such a strategy. The ability to reach across a table and shake hands on agreement is the essence of entrepreneurship and the establishment of commercial relations based on confidence and integrity. A striking example of this was our completion in four days — from start to finish — of arrangements to acquire control of the Hong Kong Telephone Company in 1984. Reference back to the Treasury and other government departments would have made this impossible, not only because of the extra time taken in consultation but also because of the inevitable complexity of political implications, which diligent civil servants would no doubt have uncovered. As it was, the deal was concluded efficiently, expeditiously and (another advantage of independence from government) without 'leaks'.

That commercial freedom, however, must be firmly linked to accountability. There are no alibis, explanations or excuses which can now be advanced, in order to shelter behind government policies, intervention or pressures. The directors of the company are now accountable, both as individuals and as a board, to the shareholders. I should like to emphasise the impact that the concept of 'accountability' has had on management attitude and performance at Cable and Wireless since privatisation.

First, experience shows that the management of nationalised industries, while technically and operationally of a high order of excellence, is unable fully to develop commercial and entrepreneurial skills and opportunities, in part because of the restraints imposed on them and in part because of the lack of real competition.

Secondly, these restraints on management arise out of the inherent nature of nationalisation and the consequent exercise of ministerial, departmental and Parliamentary responsibilites. The intervention by government in major policy issues such as investment and pricing are frequently indirect and arbitrary.

Thirdly, the objectives and needs of government, management, staff and customers may diverge or even, frequently, be in conflict.

Fourthly, profit responsibility and accountability is diffused, with adverse consequences for motivation and morale. The fact that a nationalised industry is sustained in its losses and connot be bankrupt has a pervasive influence on the virility of the enterprise.

Actions speak louder than words. Since 1981 Cable and Wireless has followed a multi-pronged strategy which would have been virtually impossible to conceive, let along implement, under the coat-tails of the government:

- it has expanded its activities in the Pacific basin, the world's greatest growth area;

- it took over control of the Hong Kong Telephone Company;

- it has recently restructured its operations in Hong Kong, merging both the national and international telecommunication operations, and created Hong Kong Telecom, the largest company on the Hong Kong Stock Exchange;

- it has established joint ventures inside China — the only foreign company permitted to operate telecommunications inside China;

- it has established Asiasat, a joint company with China and Hong Kong to provide the whole of China with its domestic satellite operations;

- it became the first British company to be listed on the Tokyo Stock Exchange;

- it has established a joint venture with Japanese partners, International Digital Communications (IDC), to provide an alternative international service in Japan: a move which is unprecedented in the history of telecommunications in advanced industrialised countries;

- it has expanded its network in the United States and now has a coast-to-coast digital transmission system in the US, where it operates in over fifty cities;

- it has installed and is operating the UK end of PTAT, the first private sector submarine fibre optic cable to cross the Atlantic;

- it is constructing the North Pacific Cable (NPC), the first private sector submarine fibre optic cable to cross the Pacific;

- it is constructing a fibre optic cable which connects up key Pacific rim countries: Hong Kong – Japan – Korea (HJK).

Combining Mercury Communications' all-digital trunk network in the UK, PTAT, the US network, NPC, IDC and HJK, Cable and Wireless will be able to provide all the peoples of the Atlantic and Pacific regions with a choice of international digital facilities for the first time in history — the Global Digital Highway. Today, the company is poised to become everyone's second carrier around the world.

None of these actions, which have transformed the business prospects of Cable and Wireless, would have been possible if

Cable and Wireless had remained a state enterprise. The full impact of this bold and imaginative strategy will not be seen on the bottom line for some time, because the capital investment required for such an undertaking is very considerable.

Equally important, however, has been the effort to improve overall efficiency and returns from existing operations: Hong

Table 10.1   Cable and Wireless financial results, 1975–89

	Turn-over (£m)	Pre-tax profit (£m)	Capital expenditure (£m)	E.P.S. (pence)
1975	110.3	21.5	14.7	2.0
1976	145.4	31.5	27.4	3.0
1977	220.0	60.9	36.1	4.7
1978	257.3	55.4	51.4	4.9
1979	301.6	62.1	47.1	4.9
1980	348.1	62.3	65.9	5.6
1981	399.1	64.1	79.7	5.3
1982	501.9	89.2	61.6	5.7
1983	578.7	156.7	70.0	12.0
1984	860.1	190.1	92.7	12.5
1985	1,105.5	245.2	216.2	15.8
1986	1,153.8	295.0	225.3	19.3
1987	1,201.1	340.5	355.3	22.0
1988	1,244.1	356.1	423.0	24.0
1989	1,534.1	420.5	677.9	27.9

Note: E.P.S. = Earnings per share

Kong and the Caribbean have shown marked improvements, and the rationalisation of effort in the United States has begun to pay off in the world's most competitive market. The financial results before and after 1981 reflect very dramatically the resurgence of Cable and Wireless since privatisation.

Ironically, the Treasury will benefit more from a privatised Cable and Wireless in which it has no commercial shareholding than it did during all the years when it controlled the company's finances. Cable and Wireless is now a major contributor to UK invisible earnings, significantly greater than it was in 1981.

11

KENT COUNTY COUNCIL

Michael Frater
Director of Strategic Management, Kent County Council

Background

Until recently there has been a lot of loose talk about privatisation and competitive tendering. Some semantic 'clearing of the decks' is required because the terms are often used interchangeably, yet they mean quite different things. At its simplest, 'privatisation' in the local government setting means disposing of *all* interests in the service concerned, not just the direct delivery of the service but decisions about the nature and future direction of the service together with the specification of service levels and standards. 'Competitive tendering', on the other hand, simply involves testing the market to find the best deliverer of one or more aspects of the service. Decisions about the nature and specification of the service required remain within the local authority.

This lack of clarity about terminology may be a manifestation of the fairly widely-held view that government policy on local government is the result, not of a coherent set of well-thought-out policy intentions, but rather an accumulation of reactions to situations in a tiny minority of local authorities. What is fairly clear is that there are a number of recurrent themes or ideological imperatives which underpin most, if not all, of the barrage of some fifty-odd pieces of legislation directed at local government over the last decade. These themes include:

- less government involvement in people's lives;
- greater individual choice;
- the role of the market-place as a decision mechanism;
- the intention to sharpen accountability.

Virtually no aspect of local government has remained untouched. In particular, the changes affecting the major services of housing (at the district level) and education, the compulsory competitive tendering legislation, and the wholesale restructuring of the financing of local government (the community charge and the uniform business rate) stand out as particularly significant.

However, there has been a subtle difference between the proclaimed intentions and the actual consequences of the legislation. The locus of decisions has *not* been transferred to the market-place to any significant extent (apart from a small number of compulsorily specified services) nor to individuals, but rather to central government ministers and their civil servants who, by definition, are remote from local needs and local markets. While it is true that a significant number of council houses have moved into the private market through sales to sitting tenants, the majority remain in the public sector. Those authorities that have sold them *en bloc* have done so to housing associations which are funded through the Housing Corporation which is an arm of central government. Schools that have chosen to 'opt out' of local authority control for grant maintained status will simply be funded direct by central government. The uniform business rate and standard spending assessments under the community charge legislation are further evidence of central government's increasing and now almost total control of key decisions affecting local authorities and services to their customers. Given the intention of this legislation to make local authorities clearly accountable for the cost of their services through the democratic process, the decision to give the minister powers to 'cap' any individual authority's expenditure is the ultimate irony.

Any discussion of either privatisation or competition needs to be considered in the context of the growing centralisation of decisions about local government services. This is not a climate conducive to entrepreneurial spirit, as events in Eastern Europe have highlighted, and it is hardly surprising that relatively few local authorities have embraced the competitive ethos and sought to change their cultures accordingly. Kent County Council is one that, despite the centralisation of key local decisions, has made significant progress in developing a more competitive culture within a local authority setting.

The Enabling Council

The idea of the 'enabling council' is one that has developed in parallel with legislative change in recent years. Broadly speaking, there are two schools of thought, the 'minimalist view' of local government as expounded by a former Secretary of State for the Environment, Nicholas Ridley, and the 'community government' view as articulated by academics such as Professors John Stewart and George Jones.

Nicholas Ridley's pamphlet on the subject painted a picture of local government where services other than minimal essential services would be disposed of to other interests, and the delivery of those remaining within local government would be delivered largely or wholly by contractors. There is little if any attention to needs and demands, or to effectiveness and outcomes. Rather the focus is on efficiency and economy, the 'how' and 'how much' questions rather than the 'why' and 'what' questions.

At the other end of the spectrum is the community government approach which focuses on community needs and interests, seeking partnership with community stakeholders be they private sector, voluntary sector or other public sector bodies. There is a focus on looking for and maximising opportunities and ensuring responsive local services. The question of who delivers the service is not predetermined, it is simply a matter of judgement about who does it best.

The worry with this debate about the meaning of the enabling council is the danger of polarisation, of people taking up fixed positions. Historically, one of the strengths of local government has been the variety that comes from its being *local*. It should be up to each local authority to decide for itself where on the 'enabling spectrum' it wishes to be, and if it gets it wrong voters can be relied upon to make their feelings known. Too much prescription will weaken local government and guarantee that it becomes no more than the local administrative presence of central government.

The Changes in Kent County Council

It is against this backcloth of massive legislative change and the developing debate about the role of local government that the changes in Kent were started. Interestingly, this was not at the behest of central government, it was because Kent's *locally* elected members (Kent County Council has been Conservative controlled for all its 100-year history) decided in the mid-1980s that they wanted to transform the organisation. Where appropriate they wanted business principles to be applied, which meant the need for fundamental change. While they were not seeking to create Kent County Council plc, they believed that the traditional professional and administrative ethos was no longer appropriate. There was a pressing need for a new vision to be spelt out; for management principles to be articulated; for the development of a new, more relevant style; for the redesign of management processes and systems; for the reorganisation of a number of departments; for new roles and relationships to be forged, and for new values and attitudes to prevail. In short, it required wholesale cultural change. To achieve this they brought in a new chief executive, Paul Sabin. He has worked in close partnership with the council's leader, Tony Hart, to lead the changes in the organisation.

The vision

This can be summed up as: 'Working in partnership with others to ensure high-quality services and maximise Kent's interest including European opportunities.' The key dimensions of the vision in more detail are:

- *High-quality public services — the top priority.* That is what the county council exists for in the minds of most people in Kent.

- *Opportunities to maximise and protect Kent's interests.* This is the active local *government* role, not the passive local *administration* of centrally determined services. Good recent examples include the response to the Channel Tunnel, the international speed rail link, the economic development opportunities which the Tunnel opens up, matched by a concern to preserve the environment for future generations.

- *Working in partnership with others.* Public bodies often work together, though not as frequently or as well as they might. Local authorities usually support voluntary organisations but in a fairly low-key way.
   Traditionally, the relationship with the private sector has been very limited. The divide that has existed (usually in

the minds of officers) between the public and private sectors is artificial and unhelpful, and means that a whole range of opportunities for the benefit of both sides is passed up. In Kent there have been significant developments in joint working with the public, voluntary and private sectors in the last three years.

- *European and international outlook.* Located between London and Europe with the Channel Tunnel due to open in 1993, Kent is the UK's frontier region. Add to that the potential opportunities and threats that the Single European Market could bring in 1992 for both the private and public sectors in Kent, and it clearly makes sense to take Europe seriously. Kent County Council does just that.

The management principles

There are three of these:

- *Closer to the customer.* This means listening to customers and then acting on what we hear. We have started this by extensive use of market research. It also means many other changes, but perhaps most fundamental of all is turning the management hierarchy, the traditional pyramid, upside down. This means putting customers and front-line staff on top with the role of the manager being to support, not tell. It means, above all, valuing front-line staff who have traditionally been the least thoroughly recruited, least trained, in the worst accommodation, least well rewarded and, if they hear anything at all, are the *last* to hear what's going on. And these are the people who deal with our customers!

- *Devolution.* In other words, getting the right balance between corporate responsibilities and service freedoms. Kent County Council, like most if not all local authorities and most large organisations, traditionally vested power and control in its central departments. They had become 'millstones round the necks' of the service delivery departments in Kent. The role of the central departments has been redefined as providing strategic direction, initiation of corporate change, monitoring and review. This requires substantially smaller central departments than hitherto. many of the professional staff, accounts, personnel officers, information systems people and the like, are moving out to be line managed in the service delivery departments. Where it is, on balance, better to keep staff grouped together at 'the centre' they no longer provide their service as of right. They negotiate a service level agreement with the service delivery department, who will have the right to buy the service elsewhere if they can't get the service they want at the price they want within the county council. All this is leading to smaller, fully accountable 'leaner and fitter' central departments. When the government makes these services the subject of compulsory tendering Kent's central/professional services will already be well placed to respond positively.

- *Management not administration.* The third principle follows on from devolution. Not only are central departments pushing responsibility for the management of the key resources out to service delivery departments, responsibility is also being pushed down the line to as close to the point of service delivery as possible. This has meant substantially reorganising some departments; others have fine-tuned their structures themselves. The purpose of these reorganisations has been to create clearly identified, and therefore clearly accountable, service or business units. In the process, management structures have been flattened with levels of unnecessary management stripped out. These changes carry with them significant requirements for management development and skills training for staff across a wide range of activities. This has been recognised and acted upon.

The developing culture

As a consequence of spelling out the vision and the management principles, a new culture is clearly developing. It has two key components, the 'core' of corporate common values, and the service department (professional) values. The corporate common values have not been imposed but rather have emerged as follows:

- *Businesslike with clear accountability.* This is central to the whole change process. It pervades everything.

- *Leading edge and innovative.* This is vital to cope with the sheer volume and complexity of change facing local government in general and Kent in particular. It is beginning to become self-sustaining. As Kent's reputation in this respect spreads, we seem to attract more and more innovative people.

- *Opportunism and risk-taking.* Traditionally, local authorities are not good at spotting opportunities, and risk-taking is allegedly anathema to local government officers. This idea is being seriously challenged in Kent.

- *Proactive, not reactive.* In Kent we want to set our own agenda, not respond to someone else's. This means going out and making things happen, not waiting for others to generate change or opportunities.

- *Enabling, not disabling.* Too many local authorities are too cautious. They seem to see their role as stopping things when a problem arises rather than seeking to maximise opportunities. That doesn't mean that there is no regulatory role, but there are may different ways in which it can be performed.

- *Competitive — internal and external.* Put simply, if we provide a service within the county council it must justify itself by producing the best quality and the best value for money. Consequently we have created our internal market, which was referred to earlier. This thinking applies to our dealings in the external market where we expect to be competitive not only when bidding for our own services, but in providing services to other public bodies, within the limitations of the Local Authorities (Goods and Services) Act 1970. If our involvement does not add value to the service then we should either ensure that it does or let someone else do it who can.

The emerging style

Over the last three years there has developed in Kent County Council a 'get on with it' mentality. Every day we discover yet more 'entrepreneurs' within the organisation who are taking risks to maximise opportunities. Action not words; fine-tune later; Ready, Fire, Aim; the 80/20 rule; all these terms are increasingly in use. But it's not all 'macho'-competitiveness, there are other equally important dimensions to the new style. There is a concern with quality and value for money. There is a developing trust and openness both within the organisation and in our dealings with customers and other agencies. Increasingly we are becoming a listening and a learning organisation.

Bringing About the Changes

Leadership

This operates in two distinct but related domains, the political and the executive. Kent's politicians have largely redefined their role as defining strategy, policy-making, and monitoring service performance. The chief executive provides the leadership to the executive arm of the organisation through, among other things, spelling out the vision and the management principles. The issue of culture and setting a new style is also explicitly tackled. Moreover, there is an explicit leadership and management partnership between the leader of the council and the chief executive. This creates a unity of purpose that is a source of considerable strength and advantage to the organisation in providing a high degree of certainty about key political and managerial fundamentals in an era of considerable uncertainty and change.

However, leadership in Kent is seen as an issue for all managers and not just for the leader of the council and the chief executive. Leadership is a management responsibility in a devolved organisation. It is clearly different from the chief executive's role, but only in degree. If managers are viewed as 'chief executives' of their unit or section or division, it is their job to provide the vision and direction and style for their staff within the framework of the corporate vision, principles, culture and style.

Effecting cultural change

This needs putting into context. Kent County Council is about three years into a programme of fundamental transformation. It was launched initially at a one-day seminar for the departmental chief officers with a firm of external consultants specialising in bespoke cultural change. They went on to run courses of some four days' duration for the 120 senior managers in groups for twenty at a time. These managers were charged with taking the process forward in their own departments. Some used the original consultants, others used different ones, yet others made use of their own and other internal resources. It is estimated now that in one way or another some fifteen hundred to two thousand managers have been through some form of 'changing the culture experience'.

A very potent symbol has been the changes at the top level. Some fourteen of the seventeen departmental chief officers changed in the first two years of the cultural change process. There have also been significant developments in management development and training. An additional £1.25 million has been put into training over the last three years, as well as the decision to provide a major residential training centre. There are a range of new initiatives under way to make radical improvements in internal communication upwards, downwards and laterally. An important element of that process, current at the time of writing, is a survey of all fifty thousand employees seeking their views, feelings and ideas about the changes so far, and what else needs to be done.

Being clear about direction

This is sometimes referred to as the 'performance requirement'. This is 'management-speak' for what do we want to do, have to do, need to do. One of the most significant changes in this respect has been the change from a supply led to a needs/demand led approach to service delivery. This fundamentally changes the debate about who actually delivers the service. Other elements of this work have included a new focus on the future by, for example, commissioning the Henley Forecasting Centre to produce a report on the issues facing Kent up to the year 2000. This is supported by a range of market research and other consumer monitoring initiatives. All of this feeds into a fairly robust but straightforward system of medium-term planning, which in turn is informed by a process of base budget policy review whereby every year approximately 20 per cent of our activities are rigorously challenged.

Managing performance

Traditionally, local government is much worse at managing performance than it is at being clear about the direction it is moving in. In Kent a performance culture is now widely accepted. Key to this is the development of business plans for departments and units. These are not commercial business plans; they are one-year documents spelling out everything that is to be done to put the first year of the medium-term plan into effect. This provides the framework for individual action plans which are reviewed through a system of performance appraisal. This has the added spice of performance-related pay which, again, has only recently been taken seriously in local government and then only at the most senior levels. In eighteen months Kent introduced, piloted and twice extended its scheme for performance-related pay to the point whereby some eleven hundred managers came within the scheme. The recently introduced 'Pay-Plus' recruitment and retention pay package extends this principle; Kent County Council is the first county council to withdraw from national pay bargaining for its eleven thousand administrative, professional, technical and clerical staff. The scheme has been developed and introduced on a voluntary basis in six months, with almost 90 per cent of staff opting in. In future, these staff will not get automatic increments each year. Their pay progression will be determined by their performance appraisal. Other groups of employees are expressing interest in the principle being applied to their areas of work.

Competitive Tendering in Kent

This needs to be put into context. While the Local Government Act 1988 spells out a range of services which must be tendered for, all local authorities have always (to a greater or lesser extent) put work out to competitive tender. Kent County Council certainly has and even before the new Act was tendering for some £120 million worth of work. One of the major compulsory services, school cleaning, was subject to tender five years before the Act came into force. As a result, Kent County Council was well placed and had already prepared its strategy six months before the Parliamentary Bill appeared in 1987.

Nearly all the specified services have now been tendered, in many cases several years ahead of the government's timetable. In an organisation that has developed a competitive culture compulsory tendering holds no great fears.

Responsibilities were clarified at an early stage:

- The corporate or central responsibility was to develop a strategic approach, ensure necessary policies were clear or modified, provide support and co-ordination and, once implemented, to monitor progress and overall effectiveness.

- The service department responsibility was to perform the client role, ensure customer requirements were known and understood, develop the service specification, carry out the tendering and contract letting process, and then to manage the contracts, including monitoring performance against specification.

- The contractor's role (in house or external) was defined essentially as delivering the contract specification, no more, no less.

So far it is fair to say that, in Kent, competitive tendering has been 'No big deal'. Significantly, it has been dealt with as a management issue, not as a political football as it has been in some authorities. A number of personnel policy changes and finance system changes have been made to enable in house contractors to compete on an equal basis with external contractors. This has not been without its difficulties, but the trade unions have taken a realistic view of the consequences of not making changes.

A number of initiatives have been taken which clearly indicate Kent County Council's commitment to the value and importance of competitiveness on both the client and contracting side.

In an effort to achieve the most competitive outcome for the letting of school meals contracts, discussions were held with nineteen potential contractors, local and national, to establish the factors which would encourage them to tender for the business. This approach has since been commended to all local authorities by the Department of the Environment as good practice. This exercise results in 160 separate contracts based on groupings of several schools and individual contracts for large schools. In order to ensure genuine customer choice in another area of activity, the vehicle maintenance contracts for Kent's two and a half thousand lease cars specify on standards of service and price, not volume of business or other measures. In each town at least two contractors (which may include the in house contractor in some locations) are approved and the one which gives the best service will get more of the business as a result of individual customer choice. To help client-side managers, the county council has made a video on how to manage contracts for use by its head teachers. Heads are at present the main managers of contracts for school cleaning, school meals and grounds maintenance, all of which are subject to compulsory tendering.

It is a little too soon to form hard and fast views on the benefits of the competitive culture in the context of tendering for work, but there are some clear indications. All 160 school meals contracts have been won by the county council's in house catering contractor, Abacus, who have also won the contracts for staff catering, police catering and fire service catering. On grounds maintenance, five out of the first six contracts were won by the landscape service in house contractor. On vehicle maintenance it is a little early to judge because of the approach based on genuine customer choice, but anecdotal evidence would suggest that lease car users regard the approach and the service very favourably. These successes by the in house contractors have been achieved on merit against two sets of criteria: quality of service and value for money. Kent's elected members would not entertain favourable treatment for either internal or external contractors.

However, the competitive approach is widely perceived to have brought wider benefits to the organisation. First, there have been efficiency savings, though the more excessive claims of the proponents of compulsory tendering of 20 per cent and more are not realistic in an authority that has a long-standing reputation for efficiency. One of the effects has been a greater concern among managers with the twin object-ives of competition in Kent, that is, with service quality *and* value for money. In house contractors are being separated from the client by transferring them to a commercial services department. One of the most significant developments has been the recognition of the central department's ability to 'make or break' in house contractors either through inappropriate policy, out-dated systems, excessive costs or unresponsiveness. The creation of our internal market has subjected central department costs to the same set of dis-ciplines. The freedom of in house contractors to buy their services from outside the county council has resulted in some tough negotiations over services and costs — a far cry from the *imposed* central administration recharges of only three years ago. There is a wide recognition that services are better managed and, in some cases for the first time, properly specified so that they can be monitored. All this has led to higher quality standards or, to put it more simply, *more and better service for less money.*

Conclusion — Issues Still to Face

The benefits of creating a competitive culture are likely to be at least as significant for the internal roles and relationships of local authorities as they are for external relationships. However, there are still a number of as yet unresolved issues to be faced. They provide an appropriate 'watch this space' way of concluding the story so far.

The artificiality of client/contractor separation

Contemporary management writers have drawn attention to the rapidly changing organisation solutions to the problems raised by the changing environments in which we live and operate. Charles Handy has coined the phrase 'shamrock organisations', and Tom Peters refers to the 'tight-loose' properties of 'sub-contracting organisations'. The 'enabling authority' is simply the public sector version, but the issues are more complex in the public sector. Developments in both the manufacturing and retail sectors such as 'just-in-time' result in a greater degree of mutual interdependence between the client and the contractor. Both have a tendency to have one foot in each other's organisation. If we apply that laudable development to the public sector in relation to external contractors there is the perennial problem of suggestions of impropriety, back-handers and the like. If the approach is applied to dealings with in house contractors there is the risk of accusations of 'fudging', of tilting the balance in favour of the in house contractor, and ultimately the risk of government intervening to have the contract terminated and re-awarded. Moreover, if the government is genuinely interested in seeing the development of a competitive approach in local government then the Local Authorities (Goods and Services) Act could usefully have some of its restrictions relaxed.

Management buy-outs — who benefits?

Management buy-outs in the local government area have been fairly few and far between so far. What is clear is that it is an area riddled with potential pitfalls, to the extent that in late 1989 the Audit Commission issued guidelines on the do's and don'ts. A fundamental question that has to be addressed is 'who benefits?' There has to be a clear benefit to the rate-payers, or community-charge payers as they have become.

There is a clear need to balance short-term financial benefit against long-term disadvantage. One perhaps rather obvious value of having an in house contractor is that there is a guarantee that the work will be done. There is no guarantee that the private sector will necessarily be interested in all aspects of council business. The experience of a number of local authorities, including those sympathetic to letting contracts to private contractors, has been that the tenders just have not materialised. In services or areas where the private sector has shown an interest, an in house contractor guarantees that there will be competition and that the council won't be subject to the risk of cartels developing.

In some authorities management buy-out might be better expressed as management 'cop-out' because a buy-out could be a reflection of an unwillingness or inability to tackle more fundamental problems elsewhere in the organisation such as central department overheads, restrictive practices, policies or systems in need of overhaul, or the wider issue of organisational culture and attitudes. In the end, if there is no competition, it is the council's customers who lose out.

The European dimension

The Single European Market legislation is already operative in this whole area of activity, and a number of European companies are competing for and winning contracts in British local authorities. What is less clear is whether British companies are competing for business in European local authorities. On the evidence so far, they are not competing much here so it is unlikely that they are doing much in Europe. If both the European Commission and the British government are keen to promote competition in the public sector they should perhaps give more encouragement and practical support to both British local authorities and companies to tender for work in Europe.

Professional services and the consequences of devolution

The next tranche of services to be subjected to compulsory tendering is almost certain to be central and professional services. The 'problem' we have in Kent is that many of these are no longer central. Finance staff, personnel officers, information systems and computing staff have been, and continue to be, devolved to service departments. This will mean the letting of large numbers of small contracts for this activity when competition happens. This is clearly an area where management consultants can be expected to show an interest. One issue to be faced will be whether to look for a 'management only' contract or to seek tenders for the full service. With the rates that management consultants charge these days this could prove to be something of a non-event. A more likely and interesting scenario will be the extent to which authorities compete for and win each others' business. That will pose some interesting management and political challenges.

Competition and responsive customer service

One of the apparently distinguishing characteristics of compulsory tendering in British local government is that services that involve dealing directly with customers have been the subject of tendering. In the retail sector, particularly the successful companies, it is usual to directly employ those staff who deal with customers. This poses a range of interesting issues. How do you specify for a customer responsive service? How do you specify for and maintain good personal service to customers — at it's most trite, how do you specify 'Have a nice day'? How does the customer get real choice?

Creating the right climate

If competition is to be more than ideological dogmatism it must lead to improved service quality, better management and improved value for money. If a successful competitive culture in local government is to be developed, the trend of less local choice and more central control *must* be reversed, otherwise there is little incentive to make competition work but every incentive for sceptical local authorities to want to see it fail. Legislative overload accompanied by a feeling of government antipathy towards local government, instanced by ministerial (and, for that matter, prime ministerial) tirades, has led to a hitherto unprecedented level of mistrust between the two levels of government. The notion of partnership has vanished. Worse, relations between the two levels of government have become a zero-sum game — for one to 'win' the other must 'lose'.

If the government is genuine about encouraging a competitive ethos in the public sector, recognition is needed that the issues to be addressed are less straightforward than in the private sector. There is a pressing need for a climate of mutual trust, confidence and respect between the two levels of government. For that to be achieved requires a less adversarial and rather more statesmanlike approach to central-local relations. A growing number of local authorities like Kent County Council are showing what can be done by local government. The ball is now in the government's court.

Most of this chapter is a factual description of what has happened in Kent County Council between early 1987 and early 1990. However, any views expressed are those of the author and do not necessarily represent the official view of Kent County Council.

12

ROYAL ORDNANCE

David Clutterbuck

If ever there were a case of an organisational bride that kept being left at the church, it must surely have been Royal Ordnance. The state-owned munitions company's origins go back as far as 1560.

Its Waltham Abbey factory on the River Lea, now an Explosive and Research Development Establishment, was known as the 'Royal Gun Power Factory' and probably supplied Sir Francis Drake with powder to singe the King of Spain's beard at Cadiz. Taken over by the Government in 1787, it helped meet the heavy demand for gunpowder during the Napoleonic wars.

Waltham Abbey was joined by the Royal Arsenal at Woolwich (originally known as the Royal Warren), which was commissioned in 1667 by King Charles II as a defence against the Dutch fleet. Over a century later, in 1806, a third royal ordnance factory was started to make small arms in the Tower of London. However, the risks of transporting gunpowder through crowded London streets were so great that the work was transferred to Enfield, as the Royal Small Arms Factory. By the end of the First World War there were some two hundred and fifty factories.

By the end of the Second World War, these had been reduced to forty-four Royal Ordnance Factories. These were gradually whittled down to eleven over the following decades. Reporting to the Ministry of Defence, the factories have had to compete in modern times with overseas equipment suppliers and the private sector to supply the British armed forces. At the same time, since 1974, when the government set up a trading fund, their products were actively marketed around the world.

Under the Conservative Government of 1979, however, the Royal Ordnance Factories (ROF) became prime candidates for privatisation. On the ideological grounds that any activity being done by state enterprises which was also being done successfully by private enterprise did not belong in the public sector, ROF was a natural early choice. With eleven factories, three administrative locations and some twenty-thousand employees, it was small enough to be tackled relatively quickly and, as a primarily manufacturing organisation, the case for private sector style management was easier to make than in many of the larger, service-based parts of the civil service. (In fact, one of the ROF factories, the Royal Powder-mill at Faversham, has claim to being one of the earliest ever privatisations, having been sold to the private sector in 1825.)

Having decided on ROF as a candidate, in 1980 the government established a study group chaired by the minister of state at the Ministry of Defence and including representatives of ROF itself, the Treasury, the Department of Trade and Industry; three outside members with relevant experience, and two further officials from the Ministry of Defence, to examine the alternative ways in which it could accomplish privatisation. The resulting report identified four routes:

- Breaking up ROF and selling it piecemeal;
- Keeping it in public ownership, while giving management much greater control over finance and strategic direction;
- Flotation via the Stock Exchange;
- Sale outright to another defence manufacturer.

Over the following six years, ROF went through a period where the only constant was uncertainty as the government tried out each of these solutions in turn.

Firstly, the Ministry of Defence took soundings to identify likely buyers for the individual factories. There was quite clearly strong interest in buying some parts of the business, but the ministry officials eventually concluded there was a high risk of being left with a rump of the least saleable and least productive sites. Moreover, any cohesion between the businesses would have been lost.

Back at the drawing board, the MoD took another look at the formal structure of the organisation. Since 1974, ROF had been run on what was known as the trading fund principle. The chief executive was appointed 'accounting officer' and made responsible for administering a set of accounts designed to parallel many aspects of private sector companies. A notional gearing was established having 'equity capital' and 'loan capital', attracting respectively dividend and interest. It had a formal profit and loss account, which the accounting officer would discuss regularly with the Public Accounts Committee, and which included a paper capitalisation of assets. There was even a dividend. However, there were still significant differences. ROF had no right to raise its own investment cash by any other route than from the government. Its opportunities to create value, in the way that a private sector company would do, were severely limited.

Clearly, there were additional steps that could be taken to make the ROF more independent within public ownership. It could, for example, be made into a public limited company, with all the shares owned by the government, as was the case with British Petroleum. Some senior managers in ROF favoured an extension of the trading fund, with further easing of financial constraints as a transitional mechanism, which would lead to the private sector.

In the end, political imperatives made the idea of long-term public ownership in this form untenable. This solution simply did not address the issues the search had started from. So the MoD moved to Plan C, which envisaged a fairly rapid incorporation and an offer of shares to the public. The prime mover was John Nott, then the Secretary of State at the MoD, who decided that the best way to cut through all the theorising and get the process moving was to appoint an outsider, an industrialist with the practical experience to initiate drastic change. Nott chose Fred Clarke, a former IBM executive. Clarke arrived at ROF in November 1982 and appointed Trevor Truman, then running an ROF factory in Scotland, to work with the MoD to establish a timetable and plan for privatisation via flotation.

One thing was clear — in its current structure and on its current performance, ROF was not in shape for an immediate flotation. It lacked a number of basic functions, such as a sales and marketing department and its own research and development activities, both of which belonged to other parts of the MoD. Explained Truman: 'It had severe productivity problems brought on in part from old facilities (some virtually unchanged since the war years), overcapacity also inherited from the war, and a lack of total responsibility for its own business planning. Despite the improvements introduced by the trading fund, the ROF organisation remained essentially a producer of products designed and sold by others. The entirety of its long-term workload therefore rested in the hands of the procurement departments within the MoD, the R. & D. teams elsewhere in the MoD, and the sales force of the Defence Sales Organisation. Investment planning was therefore severely handicapped, although when specific needs were identified, the finance was usually forthcoming. What was lacking was the ability to take a comprehensive and long-term investment view of the future trading position.' Moreover, the line managers were generally unprepared for a major change in behaviour and working practices.

The problem is illustrated by some of the problems encountered at the ROF's ancient headquarters offices in London — in the attic of a converted hotel known as Northumberland House. Truman recalls: 'When the privatisation process got under way in 1982–83, the headquarters of what was then a twenty-two-thousand employee enterprise had no telex machine of its own, no fax machine, and one primitive PC. It had no word processors in the headquarters. It was impossible to contact the organisation outside working hours except through personal contact.'

Much of the debate at this time focused on the form the transition should take. At one extreme were those who argued for the enhanced trading fund route — a single organisation with more independence. At the other were advisers who wanted to break the organisation into a large number of separate companies (up to ten) based around the factory locations.

All this debate occurred at a time when the MoD was formulating a new competition policy. Royal Ordnance faced it with a dilemma. Explained Truman: 'While, on the one hand, to take an organisation not equipped to compete for its livelihood and submit it to untrammelled competition could have been disastrous, on the other, the point of privatisation was to subject the activity to private sector disciplines and motivations. Special, but limited, arrangements were clearly going to be needed. A particular area of concern was those parts of the organisation which had capacities quite out of keeping with the requirements of the market. Important among these were the facilities for making explosives and propellants. The MoD was naturally reluctant to contemplate special arrangements, which seemed to favour a private sector company, but could not deny that a problem would exist in the short term were they not to do so.'

By this time, the minister was Michael Heseltine. He came down firmly against a strong monolithic structure, opting instead for forming four divisions, each with their own managing directors. Above these would be a small headquarters, operating as a holding company. This structure was intended to be in place in Autumn 1984, but it was held up till the next year because Parliament had such a heavy workload.

For the management team, this represented a dramatic increase in workload. As Truman explained, 'Incorporating the company was a significant event, because it required that we put in place all the mechanisms of running a plc. It was, however, still the government's intention fully to privatise the company under private sector ownership. During this time, Clarke left the company [in the Summer of 1985] and was succeeded by Bryan Basset, who had experience in the City. There is, with any company, an enormous amount of work to be done in this preparation. In the case of Royal Ordnance, this was dramatically complicated by the unique background and character of the company.'

Incorporation finally took place on 1 January 1985, with the aim of flotation in July 1986. As July 1986 drew near, top management at Royal Ordnance plc and senior civil servants were engaged in feverish activity, preparing the necessary documentation and briefing City institutions. Then, recalls Truman, 'We were approaching the final date for go or no go, when suddenly, after a number of cabinet discussions, the plug was pulled and the flotation abandoned.'

The reasons for this sudden volte-face were never spelt out, but almost certainly included the realisation that the prospectus would have to reveal the uncertainty that existed over future operations at some of the factories. Overseas orders could always be cancelled; other projects involved a degree of risk that was hard to quantify. If the newly-floated company failed to live up to its prospectus, the government would be placed in a very embarrassing position. Another likely reason was that the government also had another, much larger flotation coming up in British Gas. It could not afford to allow a relatively small flotation to muddy the waters.

Among the immediate consequences of the cancellation of the flotation was a rapid return by ministers to the earlier concept of breaking up the company and selling it piecemeal. Says Truman: 'The effect on morale within the company of the disappointment of the abandoned flotation followed by a break-up of the company would have been disastrous. Under

Basset's chairmanship, however, the implications of this course were fought through with government ministers and it was eventually decided that — Leeds apart — the company would be sold as one entity.'

By now, the MoD was left with only one option — to sell the business as a going concern. Even this proved more complicated than might have been expected when the Leeds factory, which made main battle tanks, was sold separately to Vickers Defence Systems in October 1986. Recalls Truman: 'The particular focus of attention at that time was the pending order by the MoD for the 7th Regiment of Challenger 1 tanks. I think this was for about seventy tanks and in today's money would be worth something over £100 million. Part of the arrangement with Vickers was that they received the order for the Challenger tanks. The decision to sell Leeds to Vickers was essentially a political one, although the arrangements for the sale were worked out by the managements of the two companies.'

Offers for the remainder of the company were subsequently invited from other interested parties. From an initial field of twelve suitors, four expressed serious interest — British Aerospace, Trafalgar House, GKN and Ferranti. All four went through an intensive period of briefing and studying the company and getting to grips with the various unusual aspects of the proposed sale. In the end Ferranti and Trafalgar House withdrew their interest, leaving GKN and British Aerospace as serious contenders. This remained the position up until the very end when the Government accepted British Aerospace's £190 million bid.

British Aerospace consummated the deal in April 1987. It inherited an organisation where a great deal had already changed, and which was already part-way through the transition to private sector behaviour and structures. But it was still, as Truman expresses it, 'essentially a producer of things ordered by others, designed by others and sold by others'. He explains further: 'The organisation was, of course, interested in maximising its future, but it lacked the wherewithal to do so. It had little direct contact with overseas customers, so failed to gain an understanding of the international marketplace. It had no market data of its own and was unused to dealing directly with overseas governments or with major industrial organisations overseas. At home, its product portfolio was largely determined by the MoD, with little regard for the export potential of the various designs. The MoD, in its various parts, had full responsibility for the design of the product and, when things went wrong — as they will sometimes do — the ROF organisation had little responsibility for the outcome beyond, of course, the responsibility to make the articles properly and to the intention of the designer. In the complex world of military products, this separation between design and manufacture is, in practical terms, an untenable one. In the area of explosives and propellants, for example, the process by which the material is made is, in a very real sense, the design of a product. The sense of responsibility within the ROF organisation for its operations as a *business* was, therefore, fundamentally handicapped. It had no depth of experience in dealing with commercial interfaces with customers who would look to a supplier to be responsible, not only for manufacture and delivery, but for the whole spectrum of business performance including product design, sales support, after-sales support, and so on.' The vexed problem of acquiring sales and marketing, and research and development expertise was resolved by absorbing elements of the Ministry's R. & D. and defence sales force. For example, the new company took over a large part of the Propellants, Explosives and Rocket Motors Establishment. The new sales teams were given responsibility for developing relationships with customers, something ROF had never had to do to a large extent before.

The great issue of employment terms and conditions had also been given a great deal of consideration. Because all the ROF workforce had been civil servants, they brought with them a plethora of practices that were inappropriate to, or at least, more difficult to absorb in, the private sector. There were, recalls Truman, index-linked pension schemes and redundancy provisions designed for a huge public sector organisation rather than a business operation, so that it was difficult both to move and to fire people. This being the first time that any organisation had transferred such large numbers of people from public to private sector employment, the ROF board was left in large part to make up the rules as it went. It had, in particular, to be very careful not to alter the terms and conditions of employment to the extent that employees could claim they had effectively been dismissed. In the end, a compromise solution was reached with the employees that, for example, retained a measure of index linking but with the company's contribution liability limited in any year.

Similarly, the issue of the future relationship with the MoD was of importance. Because ROF had been vertically integrated with the MoD, it had had only quasi-contractual arrangements between parts of the same legal entity. Now a whole new contractual arrangement had to be worked out, which would take into account the degree of risk. And, of course, there was a host of peripheral problems, such as who looked after sites and premises now that the Property Services Agency no longer had responsibility for them. Similarly, the new company needed to resolve the status of 'agency factories', such as the one at Summerfield near Kidderminster, which was owned by the MoD but operated on its behalf by IMI. There were also agency factories at Powfoot (operated by Nobel's Explosives company, a part of ICI) and Featherstone (operated by a part of the Sandvik company). The Featherstone site was incorporated as a new company in 1986 as Royal Ordnance Speciality Metals Limited, jointly owned by Royal Ordnance plc and Sandvik. The Sandvik shareholding was subsequently bought out and ROSM Limited is now a wholly-owned subsidiary of Royal Ordnance. The agency factory at Powfoot still operates although the agency agreement ran out in the spring of 1991, following which a new and different arrangement came into force.

When British Aerospace acquired the company, there were still a number of such issues unresolved. One concerned the placing of a major contract for a new rifle, the SA80, but an understanding was reached that the Ministry of Defence would offer the contract to British Aerospace on the same terms as to Royal Ordnance, after the sale. Similarly, British Aerospace found that, in order to make the necessary investments, it needed a long-term commitment to supply the ministry with explosives and propellants. Says Truman: 'An outline agreement was reached in which the parties agreed that, subject to certain conditions, the ministry would negotiate a multi-year contract for certain natures of ammunition.' Another issue British Aerospace had to address urgently was lack of capital investment in previous years, which meant that many of the factories needed new investment in equipment and infrastructure. But the main focus of investment had to be in changing the shape and size of the organisation to fit its new market environment. Said Truman: 'The real need in the investment area was to adjust the size of the organisation to the perceived future workload and reduce the cost base. In broad terms, this meant reducing the number of sites being operated. In the years since the purchase by British Aerospace, the sites at Enfield, Waltham Abbey and Patricroft have ceased operations and the work has either been placed with outside suppliers or moved to other parts of the company. A major rationalisation of facilities in the ammunition area has been embarked upon. These very substantial measures are all aimed at establishing a fully competitive company in the international market-place.' One major reason why much of this investment had not been made was that, before the takeover by British Aerospace, senior management had been spending virtually all its time on privatisation issues, virtually abdicating by necessity the day-to-day running of the organisation to the next layer of management down. 'It had negative effects,' says Truman. 'From 1983 to 1986, top management was dealing almost full time with the process of privatisation. There was an enormous amount of work necessary to sort out the personnel aspects, design a completely new pension scheme, and to hire advisers of various kinds in fields that the ROF organisation were, at that time, unfamiliar with, such as merchant banking, City accountants, legal advice, pension and actuarial advice. The management was also called upon to spend much time in the preparation for the government's legislation and, of course, the massive amount of detailed work necessary to complete all the preparations for flotation.'

There was also much to be done to re-educate people into private sector ways of thinking. 'We underestimated the task of changing the behaviour of twenty thousand people,' said Truman. 'The organisation needed to learn skills in areas such as international trade, collaboration, sales and legal matters, that were quite unfamiliar. In the management area, most of the management were inexperienced in running a private sector company, whatever their expertise may have been in running a ministry production arm. Throughout the organisation, the workforce were unaccustomed to the realities of a customer who might place orders, but who might not — in other words, they were not used to working in a truly competitive atmosphere in which there were winners and losers. The white-collar workforce had grown up in a regime in which they were primarily civil servants in their attitudes to employment, and this had its benefits and its disadvantages.'

Top management defined the kind of management style it needed in these terms:

- sharp
- professional
- firm (but fair)
- seizes opportunities
- to the point
- crisp
- gets on with it
- decisive
- identifies issues
- places specific actions
- rewards achievers

It organised internal training courses to help employees understand what was wanted. Explained Truman: 'In some

231

senses it was overdone, deliberately so, since it was a necessity to impress upon employees at all levels that we survived only on our collective – and therefore individual – performances. This was reflected in the personal progress of individuals. We favoured, and recruited, those who could better reflect the new culture. We changed the organisation and introduced new systems of work. We commissioned attitude surveys and instituted workshops of the senior managers to address the results. We formed teams of young managers and gave them special projects. We introduced new personal assessment methods which had a more direct relevance to the individual and the job. With all these activities one concern was that we had too many initiatives going on together. Were we to repeat the experience, I expect we would try to focus more sharply on key issues. But we did achieve a climate of change and we are certainly seeing the results coming through. It does take a long time and the effort required to achieve cultural change should never be under-estimated.'

The scale of the changes that had to be made at ROF suggests that it would take a considerable time to achieve the new management style fully. But substantial progress has been made, particularly in productivity.

Moreover, the close association with a defence firm, which already has a long and successful history of operating internationally in the private sector, has also been helpful. As Truman commented shortly after the BAe takeover: 'We have a great deal to learn that British Aerospace can help us with — their powerful presence in world markets, their experience in collaborative arrangements, the technologies they have that can be added to ours, will all serve to strengthen and multiply our common abilities. But most important, we shall be able to concentrate on the business — the business of satisfying customers.... We have come a long way from being a jobbing shop of government. We have not stopped learning, and we have not stopped improving. But we have particularly learnt that we are not in business to please ourselves, we are not in business to be interested in the technology alone, nor to produce things for which there is no market, but to build a business upon satisfied customers.'

There were, of course, many lessons to be learnt in the process of privatisation. However, Truman believes the most significant to be the following:

- Changing a non-business into a business requires the early identification of the problem and the introduction of experienced business managers from an early stage.

- The process could have been carried out a great deal more efficiently had a single method of privatisation been selected from the outset and pursued to a conclusion.

- The personnel problems of changing the status and attitude of large numbers of people were underestimated and probably will be by any other group attempting the same thing. It would have been difficult for the management concerned to accept the scale of the undertaking and the difficulties involved at the beginning of the exercise.

- The management of the enterprise needs to be seen as separately motivated from the owners in a privatisation move. Management ought to be concentrating upon privatising the business in a form that is efficient and which has the best chance of growth in the new competitive climate. Any confusion of interests dilutes this determination. In the case of the ROF privatisation, ROF management *were* civil servants and were treated as such until fairly late in the operation. A polarisation of interests inevitably occurred — this should not have been slowed down but made to happen even more quickly.

13

THE POLISH EXPERIENCE

Michael Littlechild
Strategy Services, KPMG
and Deborah Snow

The Polish government is driving the complicated process of selling off its assets. Using new methods of privatisation, based on free distribution of shares, and conventional methods of enterprise sale borrowed from the European model, the government aims to spread share ownership widely, encourage employees to become co-owners of their enterprises, and provide an effective system of controlling enterprise management.

The government has chosen a combination of giving, selling and retaining shares. It had to remain sensitive to public opinion, which was against selling off substantial proportions of the country's industry to foreign investors and favoured giving the nation's riches to the people through public share allocation. It therefore plans to privatise large and small enterprises through several different channels.

The top five hundred firms (in sales value) will be handed over to several new owners. The large, publicly-owned companies will be transformed into joint stock companies. The workers will receive 30 per cent of the stock, to be distributed by vouchers. A further 20 per cent will go to the social security fund, which distributes pensions and maternity benefits. The commercial banks are to be allocated 10 per cent, and the remaining 30 per cent will stay with the government which will decide how to dispose of these stocks on a case-by-case basis.

There are about two and a half thousand industrial enterprises outside the top five hundred list, and around three thousand in the construction, transport, distribution, tourism and other sectors. These small and medium-sized firms will each go to a single buyer.

The Communist system encouraged unwieldy, industry-wide organisations to develop. Previously, these sectors had operated in administrative units with plans from central government. Now they have to be dismantled into manageable sections. The Ministry of Privatisation invited foreign consultants to advise on restructuring and valuing key industries such as sugar, fruit and vegetables, poultry, meat and publishing. Poland's main privatisation body, the Ministry of Ownership Changes, has also set up regional offices to oversee the mammoth task.

The government has already made a number of moves towards selling off its assets. State-owned companies have been transformed into treasury-owned business corporations, and government-owned multi-plant enterprises have been split into smaller firms. Foreign consultancy firms have also been brought in as advisers.

Enterprises that want to be privatised must fulfil a number of criteria. They must not, for example, be threatened with liquidation, and must meet their liabilities regularly. They cannot hold a monopolistic position, neither can they be artificially combined into multi-plant structures. Once the government has agreed to the privatisation, the company has to employ specialists to design a long-term business strategy.

At the end of 1990 and the beginning of 1991, the authorities staged a trial run to gauge the public's desire to buy shares, iron out initial administration problems, and stimulate further interest. The first five enterprises to be sold were the Kielce-based construction company, Exbud, the radio producer,

Table 13.1   First Polish privatisations

	Total shares	Shares (public sale)	Price (Zll,000/shares)
Tonsil	1.5m	0.75m	40
Prochnik	1.5m	1.2m	20
Krosno	1.5m	1.1m	50
Exbud	1.0m	0.45m	50
Kable	1.0m	0.83m	70

Tonsil, the Silesian Cable Works, Kable, the Krosno Glass Works and the Prochnik textile company.

Privatisation day in Poland was 30 November 1990. The Privatisation Ministry took full-page advertisements in the national press to remind people of the new investment opportunities. These privatisations were financed by the British Know-How Fund. The EC and the Phare Programme are helping to pay the advisory fees.

All five sold out, creating over a hundred thousand investors. The sale of shares for Exbud ended before Christmas 1990; the clothing manufacturer, Prochnik, closed its offer on 11 January. The government offered 4 333 000 shares worth US$31 million. Each company was oversubscribed. An estimated 130 000 share requests were taken from Polish private investors, amounting to a 7 per cent oversubscription rate. The pilot privatisation project proved a massive success. Eighty per cent of the shares sold went to small investors who bought one to two share packets. The positive response was astonishing, considering this was one of the first opportunities that the Polish people have had to invest, and shows a deep-rooted interest in the concept of company ownership. 'It is a very good base for future development of Polish investment and shows popular support for capitalism,' said project supervisor Richard Wilson of the British Know-How Fund.

The distribution system was the only wrinkle in an otherwise smooth campaign. In the pilot programme, two hundred banks were allowed to accept subscription offers. This was not enough, so next time the ministry plans to allow over two thousand banks to accept the offers. Transactions during the initial sell-offs took from twenty minutes upwards as both staff and buyer struggled to understand the process. Although the first privatisations took longer than expected, in the next round the transaction time of each offer will be reduced because people will know what they are doing.

Deputy head of the Ministry of Ownership Changes, Krzyszt A. Lis, commented, 'These first privatisations are a big event in a country that was unable to organise an efficient bottle collection system for over forty-five years.' Following the first five sell-offs, the government is selling ZPO Wolzanko, Otmet Krapkowica, Zaklady Prezemyslu Tluszszowego (Fats Industry Plant) of Brzeg, Okocim, ZPO Bytom and other firms.

The Poles soon learnt that privatisation also has its setbacks. By March 1991, the privatised Krosno Glass Works planned to sack around a fifth of its seven thousand employees to avoid bankruptcy. The company, which exports more than 40 per cent of its output to western markets, had been hit by a big increase in energy costs while the exchange rate remained stable and domestic demand slackened. The sackings affected over fifteen hundred office and shop-floor staff.

Privatisation is moving ahead in other areas. Accountants and management consultants KPMG are advising the government on the privatisation of PZU, the domestic insurer. PZU is a huge domestic monopoly, which supplies almost all insurance except for overseas trade. Its position was enhanced by laws which demanded compulsory insurance of everything from cars to farm buildings. In 1989, however, the government passed legislation stating that PZU no longer had a monopoly. A new insurance law, along the lines of current EC legislation, was also passed in 1990, which said it was no longer compulsory to insure certain categories, such as farm buildings. It also abolished compulsory comprehensive insurance on cars.

Prior to the new legislation, people had regarded PZU payments not as a choice but as a tax. As soon as certain categories were no longer compulsory, the farmers, for example, stopped insuring themselves, not realising that they also forfeited their right to claim. The industry has little in common with the insurance industry in the West. It has only a tiny number of agents for the market, and insurance makes up only 1.9 per cent of the gross national product, compared to the UK's 8 per cent of GNP.

The government has allowed the industry a breathing space, but from 1 January 1993 foreign insurers will be allowed to set up companies, putting increasing pressure on the industry. In the coming months, therefore, the industry will face several new challenges: it will have to convince people to insure their cars; it will face competitors; and it will have to operate on a more commercial basis.

According to the Privatisation Act, the new single shareholder corporation is owned by the state treasury. Two-thirds of its board of directors should be representatives of the state treasury and one-third should be members elected by the workforce. KPMG's job is to advise PZU, which currently has fourteen thousand employees and four thousand agents, how to restructure itself for privatisation. It is also undertaking an audit of the business to get an idea of the organisation's financial position.

In a country which had a centrally controlled economic system, employees have to be educated how to run their organisation under free market conditions. The Ministry of Ownership Changes is training the new directors of the new companies. Foreign head-hunting firms are also helping to search for suitably qualified people to carry Polish industry through this turbulent time.

Other aspects of a westernised economy are under construction. The government is encouraging the emergence of financial intermediaries, such as investment trusts, to encourage a capital market. Foreign financial institutions are keen to help out. However, if these private investment funds are not successful, the government has agreed to establish a public fund, which will be liquidated or privatised once enough private mutual funds are established.

The French have been instrumental in setting up a Stock Exchange, because the French model of the capital and stock market corresponds closely with the Polish concept. The French model is aimed at the small investor, and has regional and central exchanges organised into a uniform national stock market. It can also operate at a low level of financial liquidity. By the end of 1991, the fledgling Stock Exchange, based on the Lyons bourse, should be up and running in Warsaw. A Securities Commission, staffed by people trained abroad, has also been set up.

Some form of voucher scheme is essential, as the population has not saved enough to subscribe for shares in the huge number of enterprises that are scheduled for sell-off. To make the privatisation process more intelligible to the public, Janusz Lewandowski, the minister of Ownership Changes, is also creating a publicity and educational programme to educate the population on the securities market. He also aims to conduct the transition as quickly as possible and decentralise the process.

Over half of Poland's retail outlets have already been privatised and sixty thousand stores are operating independently. These are usually run by the former state employees who are now operating the business themselves, or in employee partnership.

Foreign companies are keen to get a slice of the Polish cake and the government has to walk a delicate line between allowing the impetus of foreign expertise and money within its borders and losing a certain degree of autonomy. The issue of foreign investment is still a political hot potato, but at present foreign firms are allowed to take up to 10 per cent ownership in an enterprise. If it wants more a foreign investor must apply to the government, which is wary of being seen to sell out to foreigners. Despite these drawbacks, however, between January 1989 and November 1990, 2899 applications were received by the Foreign Investment Agency. Over 2400 of these were approved. Well-known companies among them include Price Waterhouse, Siemens, Toyota, Unisys, Minolta, Coca Cola, Johnson and Johnson, Hyatt, and Kodak.

In mid-1991, the Polish government was still receiving recommendations on how to implement the denationalisation of its economy. But Michael Littlechild, consultant at KPMG, foresees problems: 'This is a huge task, but the government wants to push through privatisation as quickly as possible. If denationalisation is to be successful, then it is advisable to take as much time as is necessary to restructure and build a company for its sell-off. At times, the two aims can be incompatible.'

INDEX